KU-451-705

STUDIES IN ENGLISH LITERATURE No. 28

General Editor

David Daiches

Already published in the series:

Already published in the series (*continued*):

11276

823
LAW

This book is to be returned on or before
the last date stamped below.

07 JAN

15 OCT 1992

YORK COLLEGE
WITHDRAWN
LEARNING RESOURCES CENTRE

YORK SIXTH FORM COLLEGE

LIBREX

D. H. LAWRENCE:
SONS AND LOVERS

by

GĀMINI SALGĀDO

Professor of English
University of Exeter

EDWARD ARNOLD

© GĀMINI SALGĀDO 1966

First published 1966 by
Edward Arnold (Publishers) Ltd
41 Bedford Square, London WC1B 3DQ

Reprinted 1968, 1970, 1972, 1974, 1976, 1980, 1983

ISBN: 0 7131 5107 2

All Rights Reserved. No part of this publication may be reproduced, stored in a retrieval system, or transmitted in any form or by any means, electronic, mechanical, photocopying, recording or otherwise, without the prior permission of Edward Arnold (Publishers) Ltd.

To the Memory of
My Mother
1897–1946

Printed and bound in Great Britain at
The Camelot Press Ltd, Southampton

General Preface

The object of this series is to provide studies of individual novels, plays and groups of poems and essays which are known to be widely read by students. The emphasis is on clarification and evaluation; biographical and historical facts, while they may be discussed when they throw light on particular elements in a writer's work, are generally subordinated to critical discussion. What kind of work is this? What exactly goes on here? How good is this work, and why? These are the questions that each writer will try to answer.

It should be emphasized that these studies are written on the assumption that the reader has already read carefully the work discussed. The objective is not to enable students to deliver opinions about works they have not read, nor is it to provide ready-made ideas to be applied to works that have been read. In one sense all critical interpretation can be regarded as foisting opinions on readers, but to accept this is to deny the advantages of any sort of critical discussion directed at students or indeed at anybody else. The aim of these studies is to provide what Coleridge called in another context 'aids to reflection' about the works discussed. The interpretations are offered as suggestive rather than as definitive, in the hope of stimulating the reader into developing further his own insights. This is after all the function of all critical discourse among sensible people.

Because of the interest which this kind of study has aroused, it has been decided to extend it first from merely English literature to include also some selected works of American literature and now further to include selected works in English by Commonwealth writers. The criterion will remain that the book studied is important in itself and is widely read by students.

DAVID DAICHES

Contents

Acknowledgements

The author and publishers wish to acknowledge the kind permission given by Laurence Pollinger, Ltd., the Estate of the late Mrs Frieda Lawrence and the Viking Press, Inc., to reprint extracts from *Sons and Lovers* (© 1913 by Thomas Seltzer, Inc.) and from *Phoenix* by D. H. Lawrence; Laurence Pollinger, Ltd., the Estate of the late Mrs Frieda Lawrence and Curtis Brown, Ltd. to reprint an extract from *Lady Chatterley's Lover* by D. H. Lawrence.

PART ONE

Chapter One

The chapter heading is perfectly ordinary and the opening deeply conventional. Both might have come from any one of those 3-volume novels about which Miss Prism has warned us not to speak slightingly. The opening sentence is intriguing, if not arresting. "'The Bottoms' succeeded to 'Hell Row'." But this is not a 3-volume novel and it is not long before we are aware that Lawrence wears his conventionalism with a difference. For one thing, the panoramic survey which often precedes the bringing into focus of the events and characters which are the novelist's real interest is carried out here with great deftness and economy; what ordinarily consumes half a chapter is done here in just over a page. But there is no sense of hurry or fluster either. Lawrence never loses the confident rhythm of the narrator who moves easily through a known landscape—"The brook ran under the alder trees, scarcely soiled by these small mines, whose coal was drawn to the surface by donkeys that plodded wearily in a circle round a gin"—and a familiar tract of time—

"Then, some sixty years ago, a sudden change took place. The gin pits were elbowed aside by the large mines of the financiers."

From the history and geography of the whole countryside—condensed into a few brief and vivid vignettes—the focus narrows to the single mining valley, then to one row of dwelling houses, 'The Bottoms', then to a single house, an end house in one of the top blocks. "But that was outside; that was the view on to the uninhabited parlours of all the colliers' wives." From now on, we are no longer on the outside looking in; rather, we follow what happens through the eyes of one or more of the protagonists.

First there is Mrs. Morel about whom the first thing we learn is that she was not anxious to move into The Bottoms. But it was the best she could do, and she takes some comfort, though not very much, in having an end house, and therefore only one neighbour. We meet her after eight years of marriage, with two children and expecting a third. It is the morning of the wakes, or fair. And the first glimpse we have of her husband is as she reflects "Morel, she knew, was sure to make a holiday of it." It is a hint that we bear in mind, as we move on to William, the seven-year-old filled with excitement at the prospect of going to the wakes. But is it only that? When Mrs. Morel goes down to the fair with her little daughter Annie and meets William, we realize that the boy's excitement is due partly to the heightened feeling he has for his mother—"He was tipful of excitement now she had come". Partly, this feeling is simple pride ("For no other woman looked such a lady as she did"), but there is more to it than that, as we see from the little incident where he shows her the moss-rose he had won at the fair. "She knew he wanted them for her." And when she leaves the fairground we see him watching her "cut to the heart to let her go".

As she leaves she passes a public house and thinks that her husband is probably inside. We watch with her in the fading light deepening into darkness as the revellers return home from the fair. "Sometimes a good husband came along with his family peacefully", but more often the women are alone, as Mrs. Morel is alone, and the men come lurching home, drunk and jolly. And we know that her husband will be one of these.

As we wait for him, our sympathies are with her. We may have been slightly put off by her 'superiority', but her solicitude for her daughter and tender understanding of her son are thus far presented as wholly admirable. "The world seemed a dreary place where nothing else would happen to her—at least until William grew up." We are not inclined to accuse her of self-pity, but is it too early to sense something ominous, an unhealthy dependence on her son, in that last phrase? Perhaps. But it is a contrasting note, however faint, in the sympathy we feel for her as she wonders whether things will ever alter for her and slowly comes to realize that they will not. "And looking ahead, the prospect of her life made her feel as if she were buried alive." She does not want her new child.

The heart of this opening chapter, as its title indicates, lies in the revelation of the relationship between Gertrude Morel and her husband. But once again, this 'conventional' theme is managed in a quite unconventional way. We do not get a comprehensive and minutely detailed account of eight years of married life. Instead, we start from the immediacy of the present—the husband coming home drunk and well pleased with himself, the wife waiting up for him in the silent house, thoroughly disillusioned. Their very first exchange, trivial as it is, helps to mark out the line which divides them now.

"'Oh! Oh! waitin' for me, lass? I've bin 'elpin' Anthony, and what's
think he's gen me? Nowt b'r lousy hae'f crown, an' that's ivry penny—'
"'He thinks you've made the rest up in beer,' she said shortly."

The expansiveness of the husband and the tight-lipped disapproval
of the wife are both here, as well as the contrast in accent and language
which also separates them. Throughout the book we find Lawrence
using dialogue with this kind of economy, not only to reveal character
and social origin, but also to heighten theme and relationships, yet
almost never do we feel any sense of forcing.

The narrative moves out from the scene in the kitchen into the past
to chart the various stages of the relationship between Gertrude
Coppard and Walter Morel, in a series of incidents which are illuminating without being obtrusively 'symbolic'. Though we learn more of
the young wife's history than of the husband's, the emotional balance
between the two opposing attitudes is carefully preserved. Gertrude
still keeps the Bible given her by John Field, her first young man, a
thoroughly eligible bachelor who later married his well-to-do landlady.
Here is a glimpse of other possibilities for the woman who was to
become Mrs. Morel, and her blend of regret and relief at having given
them up helps to define more closely the nature of the attraction she felt
for the gay, life-loving miner when she first met him at a Christmas
dance. So too does the fact that she is the daughter of a father "who
ignored all sensuous pleasure". She is rather contemptuous of dancing,
while the young man is known throughout the village for his skill in
it. Understandably, she is drawn to the vigorous and handsome miner,
though it is not entirely a simple matter of the attraction of opposites.
Even as she reacts against her puritanical father she remains very much
his daughter. Part of the growing estrangement between the newly
married couple is due to her persistent effort to remould him in something like the image of her father. In a nicely ironical touch we are told
that "He had signed the pledge and wore the blue ribbon of a tee-
totaller: he was nothing if not showy." What was to her evidence of
the renunciation of sensual enjoyment becomes to him one more token
of it; we are not surprised to learn a little later that he has been drinking
all the time.

The first phase of Gertrude Morel's disillusion comes when she dis-
covers that her husband has lied to her about paying for their household furniture, and about owning the house in which they live. The
clear perception of the economic aspects of personal relationships is

something not often noticed by critics of Lawrence, yet it is sharply evident in this chapter and links Lawrence with the George Eliot of *Middlemarch*. But it would be a mistake to think of these economic details as merely so much 'background'. As we learn more about the financial strain which is a constant feature of the early married life of the Morels, we begin to understand the inextricable connection between the economic and the psychological aspects of the story. It is partly the economic deprivation perpetually confronting her which forces Mrs. Morel to seek her fulfilment in the over-possessiveness towards her sons which eventually brings about Paul's emotional disfigurement.

Lies about unpaid bills, lies about owning the house, lies about having given up drink. Slowly Mrs. Morel's feelings towards the man she married begin to change until at last she comes to despise him. The final break occurs when she comes downstairs one Sunday morning to discover that he has shorn off the beautiful golden curls from their son's head. This incident is important not only because it brings to a focus and a climax the growing bitterness between the two but also because it introduces—or rather, reintroduces—the aspect of unhealthy possessiveness in the mother's feeling for her son. We see the scene mainly through her eyes, but we cannot endorse her judgment on it. Rather, we are inclined to agree with the frightened husband—"'Yer non want to make a wench on 'im'."

The scene returns to the present by way of a description of a pub-crawl made by Walter Morel and his pal Jerry Purdy. Here too, Lawrence's attitude is by no means Mrs. Morel's. His judgment on her is clear, and it emerges in explicit comment such as this:

"The pity was, she was too much his opposite. She could not be content with the little he might be; she would have him the much that he ought to be. So, in seeking to make him nobler than he could be, she destroyed him."

But such explicit judgments are not offered to us on the mere say-so of the omniscient narrator. They are given body and life in innumerable details of the developing action, such as the dispute between husband and wife about whether or not Jerry Purdy is 'mean', the evident warmth and gusto with which the two men's day out is described, and so on. And even the explicit comment does not load the dice unfairly against one character. For it continues: "She injured and scarred herself, but she lost none of her worth."

The chapter ends with a scene which we shall learn to recognize as characteristically Lawrentian, where the drunken husband pushes his pregnant wife out into the cold night and locks the door against her. Summarized like this the action would almost certainly suggest that we are to condemn the husband outright, especially as he has already been presented to us as a drunk, a liar, a braggart and a man who had no scruples about beating his infant son. But the actual effect of the scene is very different and offers an excellent example of the distinction we are often compelled to make, between what may be called the objective tendency of a given action or event and the rhetorical use to which it is put by the author. Partly it is a matter of the sympathy with the husband which has been scattered throughout this opening chapter. We remember that "He had that rare thing, a rich, ringing laugh", and that phrases such as "the dusky golden softness of this man's sensuous flame of life", however suspicious when we first encounter them, have been filled out with meaning. Partly, it is our feeling that the wife has been too rigidly unsympathetic in her attitude to her husband's frailties, that in the end she goads him beyond bearing "'Do you think it's for *you* I stop—do you think I'd stop one minute for *you*?'" But mainly it is because the interest Lawrence makes us take in this scene is not of a kind to which the question of praise or blame is particularly relevant. Indeed, this is one of the things which make the scene characteristically Lawrentian. Alone in the moonlight, Gertrude Morel undergoes an experience—a sensation?—whose meaning is unclear to her and not wholly clear to us. While her husband snores in a drunken stupor within doors, she too becomes 'drunk' with the perfume of lilies—"Then she drank a deep draught of the scent. It almost made her dizzy." And the effect of this intoxication is to drive her momentarily out of her rigid puritanical self—"herself melted out like scent into the shiny, pale air". It is not long before she returns to herself, but for us, if not for her, it is a glimpse into a way of looking and feeling very different from the confident dogmatism of her usual moral code.

Scenes such as this may be called 'characteristically Lawrentian' not only because of the comparative frequency with which they recur throughout Lawrence's work, but because they have a quality of feeling which is unique to Lawrence, and one which we respond to almost before we recognize it. By way of defining some of the elusive characteristics of such scenes, I would suggest that, in the first place, while they lie outside the routine of everyday experience, yet they spring directly

out of such experience. Secondly, they usually involve a human partici-
pant in relation to non-human life—birds, beasts or flowers. Thirdly, we
have the sense of the human personage partaking of or submitting to
the experience rather than actively initiating it. Often the person
involved is not fully aware of the significance of the experience—'we
had the experience but missed the meaning'. And finally, these experiences are not 'symbolic' in the ordinary sense, if by symbolism we
understand some sort of correspondence between two elements. It is
the reality of the experience—Mrs Morel alone in the moonlight tranced
among the lilies, bending her face to their golden pollen—which
impresses itself on us. Whatever 'meaning' we get out of it is never a
separable thing, but inheres in the experience itself. It does not 'stand
for' something, it *is* something.

   The chapter ends then, with setting and characters brought to life
and the chief themes already suggested—marital antagonism, possessive
love and the conflict between puritan austerity and sensuous warmth.
But to put it like this is to indicate what is wrong with my summary,
or any summary. For one other thing that the end of the chapter suggests
is that the terms so confidently used earlier to mark an antithesis—
'warm, non-intellectual', as opposed to 'cold and intellectual' are
altogether too crude for the attitudes to life embodied in the characters.
The warmth is as much in the woman who "smiled faintly to see her
face all smeared with the yellow dust of lilies", as in the sleeping
drunkard. Thus does the fullness of a gifted novelist's presentation of
reality constantly slip the noose of fixed analytical categories—even
his own.

Chapter Two

   We have a good idea now what the 'battle' spoken of in the second
chapter is likely to be about, though it turns out to be not so much a
battle as one more skirmish in the conflict between husband and wife.
The central incident of this chapter, as far as the 'story' is concerned is
the birth of Paul Morel, but here it is presented almost marginally,
gathered up into the larger rhythm of the Morels' daily life and the
strife that besets it. We catch a brief glimpse of him alone at breakfast,

and share his evident sensuous pleasure in his food and drink: "He toasted his bacon on a fork and caught the drops of fat on his bread; then he put the rasher on his thick slice of bread, and cut off chunks with a clasp-knife, poured his tea into his saucer, and was happy." The scene then alternates between the miner at work and his wife in child-bed. We see the near inarticulate yet quite genuine communal feeling which comes to the aid of the 'superior' Mrs. Morel, in the shape of her neighbours. While she lies reflecting that he is probably out drinking again, we know that he is sullenly at work. So that we cannot quite share her judgment on him—"What did he care about the child or her?" We sense that in his own way, even if it is uncomfortably like the way of a dumb animal, he does care for them.

Our attitude to Morel is further controlled by the little cameo of Mr. Heaton, the widowed young minister at tea with Mrs. Morel. The contrast between the thin-blooded 'theoretical' Christianity of the minister and the vigorous if crude love of life in the miner is unmistakable. Yet it is significant that it is not the husband but the wife who makes this judgment on him, again complicating the neat pattern of 'head versus heart' which the novel superficially offers—"'Yes, poor fellow, his young wife is dead; that is why he makes his love into the Holy Ghost.'" By contrast with the 'spiritual' life which is merely a blind ignorance of the physical and a pathetic compensation for its loss, the response to living embodied in Morel seems attractive.

But not for long. Morel's see-sawing between sullen dependence and defiant self-sufficiency, and his blatant plays for sympathy which even young William notices and detests diminish our sympathy for him, and we understand the young wife's need to get away from him. Out in the open meadow Gertrude experiences another moment not unlike what she felt that moonlit night when she was locked out by her drunken husband:

". . . it was one of those still moments when the small frets vanish, and the beauty of things stands out, and she had the peace and the strength to see herself." The self-knowledge takes the form of a disturbed insight into her relations with her newborn son, an insight that encompasses the novel's major theme. "Her heart was heavy because of the child, almost as if it were unhealthy or malformed." "She felt as if the navel string that had connected its frail little body with hers had not been broken". Once again, that note of unhealthy dependence, followed by something almost as ominous, a determination which implies the consciousness that the natural feeling which should make it unnecessary is absent: "With all her force, with all her soul, she would make up to it for having brought it into the world unloved. She would love it all the more now it was here; carry it in her love."

The feelings of pain and guilt associated with her sons are both a symptom and a cause of her growing estrangement from her husband. The chapter title is, after all, exactly accurate. The 'battle' itself is triggered off by a trivial incident, Morel's theft of sixpence from her money, with which he goes out drinking. Its consequences are more serious than those of their first quarrel, for she is wounded by a drawer Morel hurls at her. We are being prepared for the final "casting off of Morel" announced in the next chapter. But even this drunken brutality is not allowed finally to damn him for us. Morel punishes himself in his own sullen way for "being unable to say sorry" and we are aware that our interest is in the "deadlock of passion" rather than in the awarding of praise and blame, although we cannot fail to notice Morel's over-eagerness to escape from his problems and responsibilities to the simple, raucous world of the pub. But for all that he cannot escape, for his need of her is deeper than her need of him—"She was dead sure of him." True that she too "could not quite let him go". But "she knew very well he could *not* go". This dumb need strikes us as in some way healthier than Mrs. Morel's incipient need of her children, if only because there is no hint in it of *using* another human being. And it lends a saving grace to our view of Morel even here, where the picture darkens. His totally insincere attempt at leaving home—comically reminiscent of a little boy's, and as evident a demand for sympathy—makes him almost an object of contempt. Almost, but not quite. Something of warmth and generosity still clings stubbornly to our image of him, beneath all the shabby deception and the futile violence. We look at him through his wife's eyes—"He looked such a fool she was not even angry with him"—but we understand too, why "her heart was bitter, because she had loved him".

Chapter Three

But we sense the direction in which the relationship is developing, and are not surprised when the "casting off of Morel" eventually does take place. (Ch. III) The climactic point of Mrs. Morel's rejection of her husband comes during the latter's illness, when we see him once more in an unfavourable light, wheedling for sympathy and attention. But the break should not be too closely identified with any single event or situation; rather it is the cumulative product of a long drawn out series of conflicts and tensions. "There were many many stages in the ebbing of her love for him, but it was always ebbing." Because we have been made vividly aware of some of these stages—Morel's first dishonesty over money, his drunkenness, 'vulgarity' and brutality—the author's summing-up of the relationship does not strike us as coldly analytic. And because such comment is almost always, as here, finally grounded in a specific scene or situation, it becomes dramatic, rather than obtrusive. "There was the halt, the wistfulness about the ensuing year, which is like autumn in a man's life. His wife was casting him off, half regretfully, but relentlessly; casting him off and turning now for love and life to the children. Henceforward, he was more or less a husk. And he himself acquiesced, as so many men do, yielding their place to their children." The association with imagery derived from the seasons makes the development seem like an inevitable natural process.

"During his recuperation, when it was really over between them, both made an effort to come back somewhat to the old relationship of the first months of their marriage. He sat at home and, when the children were in bed, and she was sewing—she did all her sewing by hand, made all shirts and children's clothing—he would read to her from the newspaper, slowly pronouncing and delivering the words, like a man pitching quoits. Often she hurried him on, giving him a phrase in anticipation. And then he took her words humbly." This kind of 'telling' is surely as vivid and dramatic as any 'showing'.

As Mrs. Morel turns from her husband to her eldest son William, the boy, who has hitherto remained rather a shadowy figure, apart from our first glimpse of him at the wakes, begins to assume a definite identity of his own. Partly of course, this is simply a matter of his growing into adolescence and young manhood, for from the novelist's point of view, as from the aspiring politician's, one infant is very much like another. But the character of William also becomes real for us because we feel the tension between his mother's need of him and his own developing awareness of himself and the world about him. Her defence of the boy when his father is about to thrash him vividly epitomizes Mrs. Morel's final rejection of her husband and alliance with her son. But there is something in that defence which is disquieting, for she dominates not only the frightened husband but the growing son: "'Go out of the house!' she commanded him in fury.

"The boy, as if hypnotized by her, turned suddenly and was gone." It is she who gets him his first job, creating a further rift with his father, as it is a 'white-collar' job, and inevitably, he moves into the role which Morel has so conspicuously failed to play, that of breadwinner and responsible head of the household. At twelve he wins a race, running only for his mother, and gives his prize to her, as he had given her his trophies from the fair five years before. But for all his docility and dutifulness, he cannot find fulfilment only in his relationship to his mother, as she can in her relationship to him. Like his father, he is fond of dancing, and, we are specifically told "he danced—in spite of his mother". And the girls he meets at these dances are treated, predictably enough, with open hostility by Mrs. Morel. "Mrs. Morel would find a strange girl at the door and immediately she sniffed the air." Here we have the first statement of a theme which, we can sense already, is going to be increasingly important as the novel progresses. It is true that just before William departs for London and a new job, he burns the 'love-letters' he has received from his casual acquaintances, watched by his mother. But from the way William approaches and performs this task ("'Come on Postle'" he calls his younger brother Paul, "'let's go through my letters and you can have the birds and the flowers'") we can easily see that for him this is a mere casual tidying up of loose ends, rather than turning over a new leaf. We do not in the least expect that in London he will lead a life of austere celibacy.

I have dwelt in some detail on the twists of the relationship between mother, father and son because that is where the novel's stress is increasingly beginning to fall, but what gives this relationship its richness and depth is the vivid sense of the communal life which surrounds it and from which it springs. There is the narrower domestic circle of the Morel family—the birth of the new baby and the mother's ambivalent feelings toward it, the contrast between William, healthy and active, and the quiet and delicate Paul who "trotted after his mother like a shadow", Mrs. Morel's paper before the Women's Guild and its effect on the children. Encompassing this is the larger life of the community, evoked here in such scenes as the neighbours gathering round to help when Morel falls ill and William's progress up the social scale as "he began to consort with the sons of the chemist, the schoolmaster and the tradesmen". This alternation between the panoramic view and the close-up provides one of the essential structural patterns of the novel and in some ways replaces the traditional narrative structure of orderly sequence in time.

Chapter Four

A chapter such as "The Young Life of Paul" abandons narrative technique almost entirely, in favour of a series of vignettes which range loosely in time and place. The only real 'event' in this chapter in the sense of a unique and unrepeatable incident which moves the action forward is the return of William from London at Christmas which forms its conclusion. All the other episodes, such as the beautifully evoked scenes of Morel at household tasks (now the only link between himself and his children) are selections from a more or less indeterminate series of similar incidents. Even the presentation of Paul's illness dwells on the characteristic rather than the unique aspects of the situation: "Again rose in her heart the old, almost weary feeling towards him. She had never expected him to live. And yet he had a great vitality in his young body. Perhaps it would have been a little relief to her if he had died. She always felt a mixture of anguish in her love for him."

If we do not let ourselves be blinded by preconceptions about what a novelist 'ought' to do, we can see that this method is brilliantly successful most of the time. In the first place, it enables the author to show the continuing life of the family as self-contained and even self-sufficient, with Morel as an outsider, or at best only marginally involved. The free-ranging technique is a more convincing, and, perhaps paradoxically, a more economical method of doing this than a series of linked narrative events, which might have seemed excessively manipulated by the author. Secondly, this technique brings gradually into focus the 'special relationship' between the mother and her second son, Paul. At this stage, the greater portion of Mrs. Morel's emotional investment is in her eldest son, William, but these scattered scenes give us the sense of Paul waiting in the wings, ready to step into his brother's place as soon as the latter is absent. "But when William went to Nottingham and was not so much at home, the mother made a companion of Paul." The later development of the relationship is prefigured here from the author's viewpoint, just as Paul's attachment to his mother is presented in innumerable details, such as his presenting her a spray of wild flowers (which she accepts, we are told, in the "tone of a woman accepting a love-token"). And finally the method offers a means of showing us not only those aspects of Paul's character and personality which are to become crucial in the story that follows, but also shows us how these traits are related to the environment, both domestic and communal, in which he grows up. Thus the atmosphere of constant strife between the parents, and even more, the tension of always waiting ("All the room was full of the sense of waiting . . .") creates in the boy the twin feelings of protectiveness and helplessness towards his mother which go a long way towards defining his later relationship to her; and the longish scene describing Paul's visit to the coal company's offices to collect his father's pay brings out both his growing sense of isolation from the community and the sensitive nature which is the root-cause of this isolation. (Though we should note that this sensitiveness is not offered to us as something wholly admirable, entirely different from the 'touchiness' explicitly attributed to the youngest son, Arthur. While Paul "suffered the tortures of the damned on these occasions", we are left in no doubt as to the element of pure snobbery in his "ridiculous hypersensitiveness".)

Though the life of the family is here portrayed mainly from the viewpoint of the children, Lawrence uses the convention of the omniscient author to summarize the action, and to direct our attention to its significance with a fullness and frankness which again recalls George Eliot. We must try to distinguish between authorial comment which is truly helpful and in its way, dramatic, because it clarifies and enlarges *our* experience of the characters and situations in the novel, and comment which seems dogmatic and intrusive, an attempt to bully us into feeling about characters and their doings in ways inconsistent with our total sense of them. Thus we accept as true and relevant such a statement as his about Mrs. Morel's attitude to her husband's drinking: "The sense of his sitting in all his pit-dirt, drinking, after a long day's work, not coming home and eating and washing, but sitting, getting drunk, on an empty stomach, made Mrs. Morel unable to bear herself." And, given the relationship already portrayed between herself and the children, we are prepared to accept what immediately follows: "From her the feeling was transmitted to the other children. She never suffered alone any more: the children suffered with her." But what are we to make of this comment on the growing estrangement between Morel and the rest of the family: "Conversation was impossible between the father and any other member of the family. He was an outsider. He had denied the God in him."? It seems impossible to see in that final comment anything but an incongruous and irrelevant intrusion from the author's private 'philosophy'. Fortunately, such intrusions are very rare in *Sons and Lovers;* the author is always present, but almost always we are given greater justification for his comment than his *ipse dixit*.

Chapter Five

William has now become an exotic stranger, someone whose coming does not simply heighten the home life of the Morels, but transforms it. His life is putting down its own roots away in London, and while we know that Mrs. Morel "loved him passionately", and that he feels the pull of home strongly enough to return there rather than take a holiday cruise in the Mediterranean, we have been prepared for the inevitable transference of his mother's possessive feelings to his younger brother. Appropriately enough, it is an injury to his father that hastens and strengthens this transference. Once again, Morel's accident at work is not exploited for its uniquely dramatic potentialities, but rather for the light it casts on the relationship between mother and son. "Morel was rather a heedless man, careless of danger", we are told, "so he had endless accidents." The one that the story focuses on is one of a series— "'There's not five minutes of peace, I'll be hanged if there is! His thumb's nearly better, and now—'". The injured miner, though he is still full of wheedling self-pity, is more sympathetically portrayed here than in his previous illness, if only because we are made more vividly aware of

the reality of the pain he suffers—there is independent testimony to
this from his pub companion Barker, the hospital nurse, and from
Mrs. Morel herself. And the picture of Mrs. Morel is not as uncritical
as might appear at a casual reading. Paul sees her going to the hospital
"and his heart ached for her, that she was thrust forward again into pain
and trouble". But Paul's is not the only point of view from which we
see her. The omniscient narrator shows us the self-centredness of her
immediate reaction to her husband's accident, and the element of something like snobbery in it—"'Goodness knows what sort of state his feet
were in.'" And when we read that "It hurt her most of all, this failure
to love him, even when he roused her strong emotions", we do not
need to forget or underestimate Morel's crudeness and brutality to
wonder how much her own brand of thin-blooded puritanism has
contributed to this failure.

But the main purpose of this episode is, as I have indicated, to make us
aware of the bond between mother and son. "And they almost regretted
—though none of them would have owned to such callousness—that
their father was soon coming back." The phrase in parenthesis apparently
sets the author's viewpoint higher than that of his two characters, but
the 'callousness' is at least partly his, as is shown by the fact that Morel's
accident is presented almost entirely from outside the viewpoint of the
injured man himself.

A further stage in the link between Paul and his mother comes when,
under her guidance and control, he "launches into life"—that is, goes
out into the world looking for work. We recall how it was the mother
who had directed the eldest son into a white-collar job too. Here the
dominance of Mrs. Morel is much more evident, because it is presented
to us in a series of extended scenes—we see her almost literally holding
his hand at every step of the quest—"He was not strong enough for
work, *his mother said*" (my italics). A little later—"'Then'" said his
mother, "'you must look in the paper for the advertisements.'" To the
boy the search is humiliating and agonizing—"It stood in front of the
morning, that thought, killing all joy and even life for him. His heart
felt like a tight knot." It is his mother who scans over the copies of the
advertisements he makes and approves his letter of application (copied
out, significantly enough, from an original made by William, that other
eminently successful product of his mother's driving power). At one
stage, the author tells us of Paul, "Already he was a prisoner of industrialism", but this is another example of unacceptable authorial comment;

Paul, we are powerfully aware, is certainly a prisoner, but not of industrialism.

Balancing the growing intimacy between Paul and his mother are the brief yet intensely dramatic resumés which present William moving away from her, 'going out' with a girl whom his mother strongly disapproves of.

The scenes showing Paul and his mother at his future employer's premises and spending the day in Nottingham are presented with the freshness and evocative power we have now come to expect. But their place in the total dramatic scheme is evident in every detail. We are left in no doubt that it is Mrs. Morel who is the power behind Paul. The tension between Paul's attitude to the job-hunting and his mother's (she "stood in pleased surprise" while to him it is like King Charles at the scaffold) gives the scene a good deal of its power, while Paul's agonized effort to submerge his reluctance in order to please his mother is an effective means of conveying to us the strength of the bond that binds him to her. Mother and son are explicitly described as "feeling the excitement of lovers having an adventure together." But while the psychological interest is uppermost, we are never allowed to forget the economic realities on which it is based. William, who began by giving all his earnings to his mother, and even in London used to send her ten shillings a week to begin with, no longer does so. He spends fifty shillings on himself and buys his girl-friend a gold bangle. The breaking of the economic ties is symptomatic of the loosening emotional ones. Now it is Paul who gives all his money to his mother. The reality of these people is partly due to the scrupulous attention which the author pays to the details of their earning and spending—we know exactly how much the family gets from various sources when the husband is injured, and what these sources are, how much Paul earns and how much and what his expenses are, what Mrs. Morel spends on housekeeping, and so on. The psychological displacement of the father as head of the house is shadowed by the economic dominance of the sons, one after the other. "'I'm the man in the house now,'" Paul says to his mother when his father is away in the hospital, and though the words have no immediate economic context, they acquire one as the narrative progresses.

Paul's "launching into life" is a timid and tentative affair, but it is one of many straws in the wind. We remember how Paul had dared to disagree with his mother about the bare shoulders in the photograph of William's girl-friend. Now, as he begins work he still feels himself drawn to her ("home had never pulled at him so powerfully") and for her part, "She could think of two places, great centres of industry, and feel that she had put a man into each of them, that these men would work out what *she* wanted, they were derived from her, they were of her, and their works also would be hers." But this is not the last word here. The concluding part of this chapter gives us a picture of Paul gradually entering into relationships—"But Paul liked the girls best" —in which his mother can play no direct part; and which therefore implicitly threaten her exclusive possession of him. The life at the surgical appliance factory is undeniably sleazy and tawdry and Paul is very much a square peg in a round hole there, but as it is shown to us it has a warmth and easy-going geniality which form an attractive contrast to the hothouse atmosphere of the Morels' home life. Perhaps the chapter ought to have been titled "Paul is launched into life", rather than "Paul launches into life", but once he is launched, we can see already signs that he is ready to move out of the narrow haven of his mother's clinging love. The last sentence when Paul is described laying out his life before his mother night after night "like an Arabian nights" reminds us somewhat ominously that for the original narrator, these nightly accounts were literally a matter of life and death.

Chapter Six

In the chapter that concludes the first part, we return to William and his girl-friend, this time finally. It opens with a brief glimpse of the youngest son Arthur who is "a good deal like his father". He serves here to underline a further stage in the degeneracy of his father: "As he grew older Morel fell into a slow ruin. His body, which had been beautiful in movement and in being, shrank, did not seem to ripen with the years, but to get mean and rather despicable. There came over him a look of meanness and paltriness." The conflict between husband and wife has now become one between father and children. And in this conflict, the chief champion of the mother is young Paul. He "stuck to his mother. Everything he did was for her."

The chapter traces the gradual transference of Mrs. Morel's feelings from her eldest to her second son. This transference is charted by the two visits of William and his girl 'Gyp' to the Morel household, and the visit by Paul and his mother to the Leivers farm. The placing of this last scene is noteworthy. Coming as it does between William's first visit home with Gyp and his second, it confirms and amplifies the many earlier hints that Paul will eventually succeed his brother as his mother's 'lover'. The overtones of adult sexual love in the description of the behaviour of mother and son are even stronger here than in the earlier scene of their day in Nottingham. There is the way in which the whole ordinary world is made radiant for Paul when his mother tells him they will spend the afternoon together: "Paul hurried off to the station jubilant. Down Derby Road was a cherry tree that glistened. The old brick wall by the statutes ground burned scarlet, spring was a very flame of green. And the steep swoop of highroad lay, in its cool morning dust, splendid with patterns of sunshine and shadow, perfectly still. The trees sloped their great green shoulders proudly; and inside the warehouse all the morning, the boy had a vision of spring outside." These early scenes between mother and son have a curiously idyllic, inno-cent quality, though in retrospect they may strike us as 'unhealthy'.

Then there is the scene, heavy with the atmosphere of flirtation, where the mother puts on her new blouse for the son's delighted approval. The argument about whether it is "too young" for her is surely typical of lovers' arguments. And, on the way to the farm, he brings her forget-me-nots, and "his heart hurt with love".

The description of the farm and the family life that goes on in it is beautifully done, and while it provides a setting for the developing love relationship between Paul and his mother, in a sense it also 'places' it. The expansive rhythms and the crisp freshness of the description, particularly in the scenes involving Paul and Miriam suggest a move-ment out from the constricting home life of the Morels, even from the intense but narrow mother-son relationship. The bloom of the prose here has nothing to do with sentimental idealization of rural life; the young Lawrence knew farm life too well to yield to that temptation. When Mrs. Morel remarks "But it's a beautiful place", the farmer's reply is characteristic of Lawrence's keen realism. "'Yes,' answered Mr. Leivers, 'it's a nice little place if only it weren't for the rabbits. The pasture's bitten down to nothing. I dunno if ever I s'll get the rent off it.'"

The two scenes of William and Gyp in the Morel household serve both as social comedy turning on class differences and to bring out the novel's major theme of the mother's dominance of her children. On both these counts, it seems to me that their success is not unqualified. Compared to the fullness and vivacity with which the Morel family is portrayed, Gyp seems little more than a caricature. Lawrence does make an effort to endue her with some reality, but it is a half-hearted one: "She was really very nervous and chattered from fear." This insight is isolated and soon submerged in a kind of bullying of the character by the author. William's open rudeness to the girl is unforgivable, and presented as such, and we are presumably to regard it as an unconscious sign of the hold his mother still has over him. But Lawrence's own bullying of the character is another matter. "The young lady evidently did not realize them as people: they were creatures to her for the present." Isn't there a sneering tone in that "young lady" which is too easily arrived at? And later, having described the girl as "playing the grand lady", Lawrence can't resist telling us, what is all too evident, "And yet she was not so grand." As I have remarked, this failure in the portrayal of Gyp affects both the social comedy and the larger theme unfavourably. Because the girl is a caricature much of the point of the comedy is blunted; there is no real satisfaction in hitting a target so broad. And, with a girl so obviously unsatisfactory as a prospective marriage partner, the Lawrentian point that it is the pull of the mother which makes William draw away from Gyp, is seriously blurred. We are much more inclined to see William's hesitations and reservations as genuine and reasonable rather than as rationalizations of unconscious impulses.

The penultimate scene of William's death and burial goes a long way to amend this last defect. In many ways this is one of the most memorable scenes, in a novel packed with memorable scenes. I have already pointed out the peculiar poignancy and fullness of effect which Lawrence achieves by swooping down, from the general and comprehensive to the particular and unique. Nowhere is this effect more powerful than here. We have an impression of events moving swiftly and inexorably to their destined end, achieved in part by a vigorous selection of telling details—the ominous rash "just at the junction of chin and throat", Mrs. Morel borrowing a sovereign from her landlady and wandering about London with her "string bag that contained her nightdress, her comb and brush", the dying man's delirious ravings about his work, and so on. The death-bed scene and the burial are presented almost entirely objectively with a resolute refusal to exploit their sentimental possibilities. Even when the children's reactions are shown, there is a studied restraint: "Annie began to whimper with fear; Paul set off for his father." And again: "'And William is dead, and my mother's in London, and what will she be doing,' the boy asked himself, as if it were a conundrum." But the effect of this restraint and objectivity is not in the least that of a stiff upper lip or a callous absence of human feeling; rather we receive an impression of powerful emotions held in by immense effort. The contrast between the bald, reported speech of the doctor's diagnosis—"It was pneumonia, and, he said, a peculiar erysipelas, which had started under the chin where the collar chafed, and was spreading over the face. He hoped it would not get to the brain"—and the listening mother is nowhere stated. It is implied in the bare economy of "she prayed for William, prayed that he would recognize her", or "In the night she struggled with him." And when we recall the intensity of the relationship which had existed between the mother and the dead son, the pressure of feeling behind the 'mere' description, and the mother's repeated futile act is unmistakable: "William, when laid out, was six feet four inches long. Like a monument lay the bright brown, ponderous coffin. Paul thought it would never be got out of the room again. His mother was stroking the polished wood."

After such restrained power, Lawrence can afford direct statement and summary: "Mrs. Morel could not be persuaded, after this, to talk and take her old bright interest in life. She remained shut off." Only when her second son falls ill, too, does she realize fully the hunger for love from which he is suffering. From the time of her agonized realization— "I should have watched the living, not the dead", the transference from William to Paul is complete—"Mrs. Morel's life now rooted itself in Paul."

And so the first, preliminary phase of the novel's action ends, having given us a sympathetic yet unsentimental insight into the history of the ties that bind mother to son and a comprehensive understanding of the larger life that surrounds the pair. And we can see in outline the threats presented by that larger life to the intensity and integrity of the relationship.

PART TWO

Chapter Seven

The second part opens by extending our awareness of the life that is lived at Willey Farm, and of how that life and the characters of those who live it are reflected in Paul's consciousness. In retrospect, we can now see the first section of the novel as partly concerned with 'grooming' Paul intellectually and emotionally so that he can be not only an interesting protagonist but an adequate narrator. In this chapter we can still see the presence of the impersonal author, but the distance between him and the protagonist is steadily narrowing, and sometimes it disappears altogether. For instance, Paul's judgment that Miriam is "always sad" and that even her joy "is like a flame coming off of sadness", is independently confirmed by the author immediately afterwards, when he tells us that "All the life of Miriam's body was in her eyes, which were usually dark as a dark church, but could flame with light like a a conflagration. Her face scarcely ever altered from its look of brooding." We note that religious imagery is invariably present when Miriam is described.

Yet the distance between Lawrence and Paul Morel is important, for it assures the integrity of the other main characters, here especially Miriam, and offers us a perspective from which to view Paul himself. The opening pages, presided over by the omniscient author, give us guidelines to follow the relationship between the two as it grows to fullness. Miriam we are told "was romantic in her soul", and the scene at dinner where her brothers complain angrily about the burnt potatoes is a fairly simple ironic comment on her view of herself as a Walter Scott heroine. But even such an apparently trivial incident is subtly used to contribute to our sense of what unites Paul and Miriam, beneath their superficial differences and sets them apart from the other characters. Paul "wondered vaguely why all this intense feeling went running because of a few burnt potatoes". We don't wonder quite as much as Paul, because we are given a somewhat deeper insight than he has at present, into the girl's temperament and attitude. Her romantic vision of herself, with its emphasis on heightened feeling, and the religious atmosphere of the Leivers household are presented to us a little before they make their impact on Paul. It is just this fidelity to feeling and a potentially religious attitude to life (though one more generous than Miriam's) which Paul has too, and the incident of the burnt potatoes, where it is Paul who feels that too much fuss is being made, forms an interesting contrast to Miriam's reaction to his enthusiasm for the swing—she "was amused that he took a swing so seriously and felt so warmly over it". Incidents like these, and the scene where Paul is trying to teach Miriam algebra, give us the impression that they mean more to the characters than they do to us—but this should tell us something about the characters and their way of looking at the world; it does not follow that we have to accept their valuation of their experiences. Indeed, the full effect of, for instance, the scene where Paul and Miriam gaze silently at the wild rosebush in the deepening dark depends precisely on our not identifying ourselves with either of the characters. The rosebush is there, vividly realized for what it is: "The tree was tall and straggling. It had thrown its briars over a hawthorn bush, and its long streamers trailed thick, right down to the grass, splashing the darkness everywhere with great spilt stars, pure white. In bosses of ivory and in large splashed stars the roses gleamed on the darkness of foliage and stems and grass." But the quasi-religious experience which Miriam undergoes in looking at the flowers (emphasized by words such as "ecstasy", "holy", "virgin" and "worship") is clearly presented as a symptom of unsuccessfully sublimated physical love—"it was the communion she wanted. He turned aside as if pained." We can hardly help contrasting Miriam's desire to 'spiritualize' the wild rosebush with the direct communion of Mrs. Morel with the moonlit lilies, and of her later discovery of the scylla flowers in her garden. One of the essential Lawrentian values—one which we may crudely call a pre-intellectual relation to non-human life—emerges out of the contrast. To Paul, it is their sensuous richness rather than their explicit religious connotation which is apparent. "'They seem as if they walk like butterflies and shake themselves'", he says, while Miriam "lifted her hand impulsively to the flowers; she went forward and touched them in worship". But we understand what "made him feel anxious and imprisoned" and our apprehension of the scene as he runs in the "free open meadow, . . . a delicious delirium in his veins", is different from that of either of them.

By now the reader must be vividly aware of the part played by flowers in *Sons and Lovers*. I can think of no English novel in which they figure so prominently. It is no exaggeration to say that flowers are associated in some way with every important scene in the story. We have already encountered, in addition to the scene just discussed, the incident where William gives his mother the moss-rose he won at the wakes, that of Paul picking a posy of wildflowers for her, and of course the great scene of Mrs. Morel among the lilies. In later chapters, we shall come across the memorable episode in which Paul showers Clara with cowslips and the later one where the crimson carnation petals stream down her dress as he makes love to her by the river's edge. My earlier remarks about 'symbolism' in Lawrence's work apply with especial force to his use of flower-imagery. To be told by a psycho-analytic critic that red carnation petals are a common dream symbol for the menses diminishes rather than enhances the impact of the scene. These flowers are first and last, real flowers, redolent of the Midland countryside—campion, celandine and cowslip, apple-blossom, daffodil, gillyvor and bluebell—the whole novel is strewn with them, down to the last tragic little scene in which Paul hands the cut freesias to the departing Miriam. If they are symbols, they become so by being wholly and truly themselves.

Thus, while the heart of this chapter is the drama of the love-relationship between Paul and Miriam, we shall be doing less than justice to the subtlety and tenderness with which that relationship is portrayed if we see it as a crude opposition between physical and platonic, romantic and down to earth, religious and sensual, or what-ever—There is as much balance as mere contrast in Paul's awareness of the 'ordinary' atmosphere of his own household and the religious atmosphere of the farm. It is true that the 'turn the other cheek' aspect of religion, as it is embodied in Mrs. Leivers, and Miriam's shrinking from physical contact are implicitly criticized. But the farm is not only the place where Mrs. Leivers rules the household. It is also the place where there is "the continual business of birth and of begetting", and the scene of Paul's intense responsiveness to natural life, a responsiveness which awakens a kindred warmth in Miriam, however much she intellectualizes it. Undoubtedly there is a conflict between the two; but their mutual attraction is the result of each recognizing in the other something of himself or herself.

There are two ways in which we are invited to look at the conflict between the lovers. On the one hand, there is the frustration caused

by the denial of the physical element in the relationship. This denial
as I have suggested, is not to be located entirely in Miriam's religious
inhibition. There is nothing so coarse here as male importunity versus
female resistance. We remember the earlier statement of the same theme
in the Gertrude–Walter Morel relationship as we realize that the
tendency to make the relationship 'abstract' (one of Lawrence's favourite
hate-words) is Paul's as much as Miriam's. He too shrinks from her
physical touch—"if she put her arm in his, it caused him abrupt physical
torture"—and suffers from a 'split consciousness'—"He was one inter-
necine battle, and he became cruel to her because of it."

On the other hand, we see Paul as the prize for which two women,
his mother and Miriam, struggle, or perhaps more accurately, as the
battleground for their struggle. On this view (which of course recapitu-
lates the earlier story of William, Gyp and Mrs. Morel) the Paul–
Miriam relationship is doomed because Paul is too much enclosed in
the cocoon of his mother's protectiveness. (This, incidentally, is substantially the picture presented in the real-life 'Miriam's' own account
of her early relationship with Lawrence, published under the title
D. H. Lawrence, A Personal Record—by E.T.) And the brooding jealous
presence of the mother is powerfully evident in this chapter. The
relationship between Miriam and Mrs. Morel flares into open dislike
after a number of "tiny insults" and when Miriam stops seeing Paul
on Thursday evenings "Mrs. Morel sniffed with satisfaction at this
arrangement" (we may remember the same telling word used when she
"sniffed the air" when one of William's new-found girl-friends called
at the house—it is one of Mrs. Morel's mannerisms). More significantly,
the physical contact from which he shrinks with Miriam comes easily
enough when he is with his mother; "He kissed her forehead that he
knew so well: the deep marks between the brows, the rising of the
fine hair, greying now, and the proud setting of the temples. His hand
lingered on her shoulder after his kiss. Then he went slowly to bed.
He had forgotten Miriam; he only saw how his mother's hair was
lifted back from her warm broad brow. And somehow, she was hurt."
Perhaps we should not make too much of this. Yet, its cumulative effect
seems to reinforce the theme of the mother as sexual competitor, especially when taken together with the unmistakable sexual overtones in the
arguments over Miriam between mother and son, and the unconscious
irony in Mrs. Morel's comment on the girl: "'She is one of those who
will want to suck a man's soul out till he has none of his own left.'"

The two aspects of the love-relationship are of course connected. And the revelation of this love, constricted on one side by the possessive demands of a rival, tormented on the other by its own consciousness of guilt is slow, painful and utterly convincing. Very rarely, the author's summary strikes us as too glib. "In contact with Miriam, he gained insight; his vision went deeper. From his mother he drew the life-warmth, the strength to produce; Miriam urged this warmth into intensity like a white light." But most of the time, whether in scene or summary, the frustration of physically repressed love is presented with tenderness and unsparing clarity. And the author's attitude to Paul is not so protective that it distorts our view of what is happening. Paul's cruelty and insensitivity to Miriam's suffering is fully faced. "'I can't help it,' he said rather pitiably", when Miriam's mother asks him not to be too hard on her, and in the ambiguity of that single word 'pitiably' (pathetic/contemptible) we sense the balance and control in the author's view of his hero. Even more severe is this judgment on Paul, though the context does not make it absolutely clear whether it comes from Miriam or Lawrence himself—"He was a fool who did not know what was happening to himself." The charge sometimes made against Lawrence that he protects his hero while he bullies other characters is least true here.

Chapter Eight

Though it is clear now that the twin themes of Paul's development as an artist and his sexual development, and the relationship between these two are the novel's main concern, they are never treated in isolation. We are always aware of the ordinary routine of domestic and social life within which the chief characters work out their destiny. Thus in a chapter where the sexual struggle is more explicit than it has been so far, we find two long scenes, which may appear to be extraneous to the main story. The first, which opens the chapter, deals with the escapade which ends in the youngest son Arthur taking the King's shilling. The treatment of Arthur and his history not only in this scene but throughout the book is a good example of the novelist's skill in subordinating our interest in the minor characters without turning them into lifeless puppets obviously manipulated in the interests of some abstractly conceived 'theme'. We know enough about Arthur to make him real and convincing—his similarity to his father, his recklessness, his inability to keep a job, and so on. Yet what we know casts its own oblique but needful light on the changing pattern of relationships between the main characters. We understand Arthur's frequent nights out all too easily as an escape from a homelife in which neither mother nor father seem to take very much notice of him. His fondness for girls hardly needs any special explanation. But it is the mother, not the father, who first goes down to the recruiting office to try and get him out—which confirms our impression of this woman whose life is now wholly in her children, and whose will gives the family what coherence it has. The touch of snobbery we had earlier encountered is still there ("'a common soldier!'") and is a point of difference between herself and Paul—or so Paul would like to think. But perhaps more important is the brief exchange between Paul and Mrs. Morel about her feelings for Arthur: "'Are you fearfully fond of him?' Paul asked his mother. 'What do you ask that for?' 'Because they say a woman always likes the youngest best.' 'She may do—but I don't. No, he wearies me.'" The significance of this is not so much in what it tells us about Mrs. Morel and Arthur, but in the light it sheds on her relationship to Paul. The extreme candour of her reply on such a topic suggests that she hardly regards Paul as a son at all, but more as the head of the household, and perhaps as something more, something which comes more and more to the surface as the chapter progresses.

The other apparently extraneous scene is the one showing Morel at home, sharing out the week's takings with his fellow workers. One obvious function of this episode is to provide, in a convincingly dramatic form, that background of economic reality which, as I have already suggested, is to Lawrence an important aspect of the truth of fiction and one which his critics have underestimated. The brief glimpse of the unspoken but genuine companionship of men at work also provides a contrast to the somewhat claustrophobic atmosphere of Paul's relationship with his mother. And Morel's preoccupation with warmth in the literal sense, ludicrous as it is, reminds us that 'warmth' is one of the values linked with him and conspicuously absent from his wife.

The "strife in love" to which the chapter title directs our attention has several aspects. First and most evident is the conflict between Mrs. Morel and Miriam for Paul's affections, seen mainly through the bitter

self-delusion of Mrs. Morel herself. She is deluded, first, in believing that
Paul is in love with Miriam and more grievously in the lack of understanding (we have already seen it in one of her earlier comments) which
makes her attribute to Miriam her own vampiric hold over Paul:
"'She wants to draw him out and absorb him till there's nothing left of
him, even for himself. He will never be a man on his own feet—she
will suck him up.'"

But is she self-deluded? Barely a page after this comment, the author
in his own person sums up Miriam's effect on Paul: "She did not want
to meet him so that there were two of them, man and woman together.
She wanted to draw all of him into her." I can only say that this does
not accord with my sense of the relationship as it is presented. Nor is it
easily reconcilable with other authorial comments on the same scene:
"He wanted now to give her passion and tenderness, and he could not."
"And he knew he was as much to blame himself."

The strife between the two women is reflected in the agonizing self-
division within Paul himself. His lack of insight into the truth of his
relationship with his mother forces him into emotional cruelty and
insensibility to Miriam. There is a revealing moment when, after Paul
has suggested that perhaps Miriam likes Clara Dawes because she has a
grudge against men, the author comments: "That was more probably
one of his own reasons for liking Mrs. Dawes, but this did not occur
to him." Thus, in addition to the conflict between Miriam and Mrs.
Morel and the division within Paul himself, "Strife in love" has the
third aspect, hinted at here, of Miriam's jealousy of other women and,
over-arching all those, a powerful but unclear awareness of an opposition between physical and spiritual love.

One image for this opposition is the sense of strain in the scene where
we are told about the young people's religious struggles and the later
one where Paul reads through and corrects Miriam's French journal.
In E.T.'s memoir which I have referred to earlier, there is a full and
vivid account of the intellectual development of Lawrence and 'Miriam'
We learn about the books they read together, and the details of the
arguments they had. In the novel, however, we have a single paragraph
beginning "At this time he was beginning to question the orthodox
creed". It goes on to say that "with an intellect like a knife the man she
loved examined her religion in which she lived and moved and had her
being". Are we justified in asking for more than this, for some evidence
of the actual operation of this knife-like intellect (such as, for instance

we find in Joyce's *Portrait of the Artist As A Young Man*)? Perhaps we are, in so far as the novel purports to give us Paul's development as an artist (though this takes place without strictly *intellectual* growth, in the narrower sense).

But here quite evidently the argumentation is a dramatic device to underscore a certain aspect of the relationship. Intellectual cruelty is one way in which Paul 'gets at' Miriam to compensate for the denial of the body. She wants to possess *his* soul, so in revenge "he was even more fierce, as if he would kill her soul". Similarly, behind Miriam's stiff and halting French, we sense the reality of her feelings for Paul, feelings which he himself is compelled to acknowledge, however deviously—"He only knew she loved him. He was afraid of her love for him. It was too good for him, and he was inadequate." While Paul tries to evade the sexual responsibilities of his relationship to Miriam by assuming the role of teacher, Miriam, consciously or not, circumvents his scheme by turning her journal into a scarcely-disguised love-letter.

The contrast we have already seen, between the physical unease of Paul and Miriam and the physical intimacy of son and mother becomes nakedly explicit here. When Miriam lays her hand on his forehead (the first definite physical contact between them) Paul feels "His body was somewhat discarded", and later, "he knew, before he could kiss her, he must drive something out of himself". In the scene with his mother which closes the chapter (and in which the rivalry between father and son flares into something very near open physical hostility), every word and gesture is heavy with physical intimacy. (It is characteristic of the novel that the occasion should be so trivial a matter as the accidental burning of a loaf of bread.)

"'And I've never—you know, Paul—I've never had a husband—not really—.' He stroked his mother's hair, and his mouth was on her throat." And after the quarrel with his father, Paul is insistent in his demand that his mother sleep in his sister's bed, not with his father. Paul's feeling for Miriam, intensely as he feels her presence, pales beside the passionate bond which draws him to his mother and her to him. It gives him solace and a certain strength, but of an ambiguous kind—"he was at peace because he still loved his mother best. It was the bitter peace of resignation."

Few readers will be surprised to see that the next chapter is entitled "Defeat of Miriam".

NUNTHORPE GRAMMAR SCHOOL LIBRARY, YORK

Chapter Nine

This chapter, as the author himself tells us, concludes a phase in Paul's emotional development. But it also marks the beginning of another. The rich yet ultimately frustrating love affair with Miriam drags nearer to its inevitable end as both parties come to realize that no closer or more permanent union is possible than that which they have already achieved. Each attributes the failure to a different motive—Paul to Miriam's ceaseless desire to "'absorb, absorb, as if you must fill yourself up with love, because you've got a shortage somewhere'", Miriam to the inordinate influence of Paul's mother. And as readers we are made to see that these motives are not mutually exclusive. The kind of wide-ranging and sympathetic insight which we are offered is designed, among other things, to prevent us from putting the blame on one side rather than another (though we are still disturbingly aware of the discrepancy between the author's attitude to the mother and the effect of her realized presence). In the scene where Miriam is kissing the daffodils (another crucial flower scene) Paul upbraids her in terms which are little more than a rationalization of his own inability to love: "'You're always begging things to love you,' he said, 'as if you were a beggar for love. Even the flowers, you have to fawn on them—.'" Our perspective on this is indicated by the author's comment "He had not the faintest notion of what he was saying." In other words, we have an insight into his cruelty which Paul does not have, or has only intermittently.

The quickening life of the world in springtime, with its traditional associations as the setting for the burgeoning of young love forms a poignantly ironic setting for this particular pair of young lovers whose love begins to wither away before it has ever begun to flower. The beautiful descriptions of things in flower—daffodil, lilac, cowslip—which should be emblems of the blossoming love make it instead more pathetic by contrast. It is not Miriam but Clara whom Paul decks with flowers, the beautiful, brittle woman whose cold insouciance gives Paul such welcome relief from the intense possessiveness of Miriam. And the overtones of the words he utters as he does so suggest the hollow deadness of the attraction between them:

"'Ashes to ashes, and dust to dust,
  If the Lord won't have you, the devil must.'
  The chill flowers fell on her neck."

Paul is drawn to Clara Dawes simply because she doesn't seem to care about men (as the author has hinted in the earlier chapter). She *appears* to be more interested in a horse than she would ever be in a man. At first Paul calls her "Mrs. Nevermore" and can't stand her, but something makes him insistently seek her attention. And of her we learn that "She turned her back on him. Yet everybody could see that the only person she listened to, or was conscious of, was he, and he of her." Beneath her apparent hostility to men we sense a deep hunger. Clara Dawes is, in her own way, as much in danger of "going dotty with being too lonely" as poor, effusive Miss Limb of whom Clara herself says "I suppose she wants a man".

It is significant that Mrs. Morel is far more tolerant of the new relationship which we see forming between her son and Clara than she ever was of that between Paul and Miriam. She herself is not very clear why: "She would have been glad now for her son to fall in love with some woman who would—she did not know what. . . . She wished he knew some nice woman—she did not know what she wished, but left it vague. At any rate she was not hostile to the idea of Clara." But we can hardly miss seeing that Mrs. Morel is content to let the new affair take its course because she senses instinctively from the way her son talks about her—"'she's nice. And she seems straight, you know—not a bit deep, not a bit.'"—that her own sovereignty over him is not threatened.

Thus, presided over by the brooding figure of the mother, Paul's feeling for Miriam is slowly denuded of almost everything but intellectual companionship, while the frustrated physical aspect of that relationship is trivialized and rendered comparatively harmless in being transferred to Clara. (The submerged sexual overtones in the lines which tell us of the change are significant: "Miriam was the threshing floor on which he threshed out his beliefs. While he trampled his ideas upon her soul, the truth came out for him. She alone was his threshing floor.")

By contrast we are offered the blatant but wholesome sexuality of the brief scene between the younger brother Arthur (a dashing figure—ideal for the conventional 'hero'—in his scarlet and yellow army uniform) and his girl-friend, Beatrice: "Deliberately, and with a peculiar quivering smile that seemed to overspread her whole body, she put her mouth on his. Immediately his arms folded round her. As soon as the long kiss was finished she drew back her head from him, put her delicate fingers on her neck, through the open collar. Then she closed her eyes, giving herself up again in a kiss.

"She acted of her own free will. What she would do she did, and made nobody responsible."

The final comment—obviously the author's—is perhaps intended in the first place to point a contrast to Miriam, but its implications apply at least as much to Paul.

The other scene of overt sexual feeling is, characteristically enough, that between Paul and his mother when he takes her to Lincoln. "'You forget I'm a fellow taking his girl for an outing.'" retorts Paul when Mrs. Morel complains that he is spending too much money. He buys her flowers, takes her to an expensive restaurant and talks to her in terms which lovers use. "'Why can't a man have a young mother?'" he finally blurts out (and the ensuing dialogue is an ominous hint of the illness which is beginning to cast its long shadow). And for her part she tacitly accepts the sexual aspect of their relationship. On her own admission she is readier to let Annie get married, and Arthur slip away from her than lose Paul to another woman. Even to herself, as we saw, she cannot bear to think clearly about what kind of woman would really suit Paul. "'And you think I'd let a wife take me from you?'" Paul says to her while they are discussing Annie's marriage (for all the world like husband and wife), and though she protests, she protests very feebly indeed.

So that we have no choice but to read some irony into Paul's summing-up of his own feelings which concludes the chapter: "But he belonged to Miriam. Of that she was so fixedly sure that he allowed her right." The contrast he has in mind is between his feelings for Clara and for Miriam, but we can hardly miss being reminded of the really important woman in his life.

Chapter Ten

Mrs. Morel is as firmly in control of Paul's artistic as of his emotional development. When the news comes that he has sold a painting and won a prize, her excitement almost frightens him (even the postman comes running back to see what's happened). "'I knew we should do it,'" she keeps repeating. We see her resolutely building him up in the image of her dead son, refashioning William's clothes so that Paul may wear them. "And as she smoothed her hand over the silk collar she thought of her eldest son. But this son was living enough inside the clothes. She passed her hand down his back to feel him. He was alive and hers. The other was dead."

Because his growth as an artist is so completely contained within this possessiveness, Mrs. Morel is not only willing but eager to see Paul moving in the new social circles to which he now has the entrée—"new friends who had dinner at seven-thirty in the evening". There follows a revealing exchange on class in which Paul's pretensions to emancipation are neatly deflated by his mother—but not quite. We feel not so much that the young man is mistaken in his view that "'the difference between people isn't in their class, but in themselves'", but that he does not yet have sufficient experience of what is really implied in this insight, which certainly reveals an attitude more generous than that underlying Mrs. Morel's ambition—"She frankly wanted him to climb into the middle classes, a thing not very difficult, she knew." Against this, Paul's stumbling insistence on "life itself—warmth" recalls to us his father in him, the father who has now shrunk into a shadow—"only Morel remained unchanged, or rather, lapsed slowly".

Under Mrs. Morel's complaisant eye, Paul's liaison with Clara Dawes gains in strength and intimacy. As a prelude to it we are offered Mrs. Morel's view of Miriam and her role which is substantially that of her son, and of the author himself: "Mrs. Morel felt as if her heart would break for him. At this rate she knew he would not live. He had that poignant carelessness about himself, his own suffering, his own life, which is a form of slow suicide. It almost broke her heart. With all the passion of her strong nature she hated Miriam for having in this subtle way undermined his joy. It did not matter to her that Miriam could not help it. Miriam did it, and she hated her." This is far more acceptable as the biased view of an anguished mother who has already lost one son and is afraid for the other, than as the generalized comment of the author. Earlier (after an argument over the relative importance of a full' life as against a happy one), the author tells us that "struggles of this kind often took place between her and her son, *when she seemed to fight for his very life against his own will to die*" (my italics). While there is a kind of irony to which we respond in this picture of the dying mother fighting to restore the will to live in her son, it seems to me that we have here another instance of authorial comment which runs counter to our understanding of the characters and their situation. If Paul really is losing his will to live nothing in our view of Miriam suggests that she alone was responsible for this. (It seems clear that in the words "It did not matter to her that Miriam could not help it", the author is implicitly endorsing the mother's view.)

What is triumphantly achieved in this chapter is the characterization of Clara Dawes—the 'new' woman, intelligent, economically independent and emancipated, yet with an emotional hunger not the less deep for being unacknowledged or disguised as hostility to men. The alternating current of attraction and repulsion between herself and Paul is beautifully presented in a series of scenes which are in themselves slight but which together greatly illuminate our understanding not only of the individual characters but of their relationship to each other and to the world about them. On his first visit to her home, Clara's mother says "'A house o' women is as dead as a house wi' no fire, to my thinkin'. I'm not a spider as likes a corner to myself'", and we feel that the daughter's sentiments, if she would only avow them, would not be very different. At any rate, it is at some such realization about her that the hero arrives, after a series of contretemps. When he first sees her at home, "It seemed as if she did not like being discovered in her home circumstances." At the end of the chapter she is not only telling him the story of her broken marriage but diagnosing, with an acuteness to which we assent even if Paul doesn't, exactly what is wrong in his relationship with Miriam. His view of Clara to begin with is not different from that of the work-girls (though their *attitudes* vary—he being attracted, they put off). There is a remote dignity about her which reminds him "of Juno dethroned" and which Fanny the hunchback calls "'think(ing) yourself a fine figure in marble, and us nothing but dirt'". The difference is that he senses instinctively that there is more to her than this, and is sufficiently attracted to her to find out. But for some time he lacks confidence in the rightness of his instinctive judgment, and this gives a see-saw inconsistency to his behaviour toward her. First he is rude to her, then he offers her chocolates, then he is upset because she doesn't eat them at once. On his birthday they walk up to the Castle and achieve a few moments of quiet happiness, but again he disturbs this by talking about it and making explicit contrasts between Clara and the other work-girls.

Slowly the relationship grows to maturity till they can freely exchange emotional confidences with each other. But we feel the absence of the depth of feeling which marked Paul's relationship with Miriam, and he feels it himself: "He talked to her now with some of the old fervour with which he had talked to Miriam but he cared less about the talk; he did not bother about his conclusions." We can understand why the mother is quite content to let this liaison take its own course.

Clara's independence of judgment also offers us a perspective on Paul different from his mother's uncritical adulation. She is critical of him both as man and as artist: "'You are affected in that piece,' she would say; and, as there was an element of truth in her condemnation, his blood boiled with anger." And at the end, she resolutely refuses to accept his (and his mother's) view of Miriam's attitude: "'She doesn't want any of your soul communion. That's your own imagination. She wants you.'" This lets in a much needed draught of fresh, cold air, for something like it is surely very close to our own impression of Miriam thus far, in spite of the insistent association with her of 'religious' epithets. Conversely, Miriam's judgment on his affair with Clara corresponds fairly closely to our own: "Miriam knew now how strong was the attraction of Clara for him; but still she was certain that the best in him would triumph. His feeling for Mrs. Dawes—who, moreover, was a married woman—was shallow and temporal, compared with his love for herself. He would come back to her, she was sure." If we suspect that her last hope will prove delusory, it is because we are in a better position to feel just how strong a grip his mother has over Paul. But, discounting the prim little parenthesis, we are inclined to accept the rest of her account. The concluding pages of this chapter offer a good example of the author's firm control over the hero—our experience and judgment is *not* co-extensive with Paul's nor is it intended to be (see for instance, the numerous comments such as "He could feel, but he could not understand", "He did not at all see", "He saw none of the anomaly of his position", etc.).

The surrounding life, meanwhile, is presented in vivid, yet economical summary. A single sentence shows us the ageing Morel—"His father, getting an old man, and lame from his accidents, was given a paltry poor job"—while a paragraph tells us of Arthur's enforced marriage, his temporary rebellion and his subsequent acceptance of his domestic responsibilities. Not the least impressive thing about *Sons and Lovers* is the author's almost unfailing sense of what is important to the development of his theme. Lawrence is able to summarize a whole family history in a paragraph, yet he will take pages to tell us the fate of three chocolate creams, and make us see that the last is more important to our understanding.

Chapter Eleven

Painfully, like a wounded animal, the affair with Miriam limps on to its foredoomed end. What prevents it from seeming tedious or sentimental is Lawrence's masterly control of the various points of view from which the story is told. It is of course, primarily Paul's story; but we are not asked to accept Paul's version of it as the whole truth. Nor, though we feel the presence of the mother as keenly as ever, is her angle on events presented as definitive. Miriam too is made to shed her own particular light on what happens, and above and beyond all these, we are aware of the presence of the author himself, guiding our sympathies and interests now to this aspect of the relationship, now to that. (By 'the author' I do not necessarily mean the historical D. H. Lawrence, but rather the figure who is *implied* as our guide, philosopher and friend through this particular narrative; whether this figure corresponds at all points to the historical one is irrelevant. See the illuminating remarks on this topic in pp. 71–6 of Wayne Booth's *The Rhetoric of Fiction*.)

The chapter opens with Paul taking stock of his emotional situation. Most of the opening reflections are to be attributed to Paul himself, and are an indication of his growing maturity, his capacity to look critically at himself. His diagnosis in himself of "overstrong virginity", his shrinking from physical contact (which he is honest enough to see in himself as well as in Miriam) and his growing awareness of his mother's hold over him ("he could not have faced his mother", unless he married the right woman) are all aspects of his experience and temperament which have been fully realized for us. He himself, it is worth noting, sees this as part of a general condition rather than an individual predicament:

"A good many of the nicest men he knew were like himself, bound in by their own virginity, which they could not break out of. They were so sensitive to their women that they would go without them forever rather than do them a hurt, an injustice. Being the sons of mothers whose husbands had blundered rather brutally through their feminine sanctities, they were themselves too diffident and shy. They could easier deny themselves than incur any reproach from a woman; for a woman was like their mother, and they were full of the sense of their mother. They preferred themselves to suffer the misery of celibacy rather than risk the other person."

Beginning with Paul's own assessment, this passage seems to move out into the author's generalizing judgment. The smoothness of the change (the tone hardly alters) suggests a degree of identification between Paul and the author which critics too much aware of the novel's auto-biographical origin, tend to over-emphasize. In this particular instance, in the absence of any direct presentation of the other "nice young men" spoken of, we are justified in seeing the comment as an instance of authorial special pleading for the protagonist. But such instances are rarer than many critics would lead us to suppose.

In the scenes showing the love-making of Paul and Miriam, for instance—surely among the most poignant in modern fiction, with their haunting sense of the utter discrepancy between physical consummation and true human fulfilment, the sexual union between the lovers marking the nadir rather than the zenith of their relationship—we are not allowed to forget how much Paul contributes to the total failure:

"He seemed to be almost unaware of her as a person: she was only to him then a woman."

And his horror at the realization that "she had not been with him all the time" during the physical union is ironically qualified by the reader's awareness that he himself had been less than fully present ("He could not meet her gaze", "His eyes, full of the dark, impersonal fire of desire, did not belong to her"). This sense of her remoteness during the physical act degenerates first into something very like male pique:

"'You are sure you want me?' he asked, as if a cold shadow had come over him.

'Yes, quite sure.'" (And a few lines later:)

"He had almost wilfully to put her out of court, and act from the brute strength of his own feelings. And he could not do it often, and there remained afterwards always the sense of failure and of death."

Finally, it becomes the most blatant kind of rationalization and self-deception, but the hero's, rather than the author's. With all his growth in critical detachment toward himself, the full meaning of this ending love is something he cannot yet recognize. It is not only this kind of simple psychological compensation that we are here concerned with: "He knew he had landed her in a nasty hole, and was leaving her in the lurch. It angered him"—but the deeper distortion involved in: "At last the whole affair appeared in a cynical aspect to him. She had really played with him, not he with her"—and the need for self-justification which makes him say to his mother, about the end of the affair: "'She never thought she'd have me, Mother, not from the first, and so she's not disappointed.'" Recalling Miriam's original remarks and their context, we realize the injustice of Paul's summary and the extent of his self-deception. And the author's awareness of what is happening is clear when he tells us of his hero that "In the reaction towards restoring his self-esteem, he went into the Willow Tree for a drink", and that a few hours after the great break, "He had forgotten Miriam now."

If Paul's view of his affair with Miriam is a poor indication of his understanding of himself, a much more favourable one is offered by his changing relationship with his mother. As he grows more independent and critical of her, she instinctively loses her confidence in her capacity to hold him: "She recognized, however, the uselessness of any further interference. He went to Willey Farm as a man now, not as a youth. She had no right over him. There was a coldness between him and her. He hardly told her anything." The hint, in the closing sentence of the paragraph from which I have just quoted, of the link between Mrs. Morel's physical health and her hold over her son is important for Lawrence's original theme: "Mrs. Morel was tired. She began to give up at last; she had finished. She was in the way." We are not shown this change in Mrs. Morel actually taking place; it is presented as accomplished fact. The effect is to make it seem as automatic as the movement of a pulley; as soon as Paul faces up frankly to the fact of his physical manhood, his mother's grip over him loosens. Even when he tells her he is about to break with Miriam, he does not need the accustomed solace from her: "'Never mind, my son,' she said, 'you will be so much better when it is all over.'

"Paul glanced swiftly at his mother in surprise and resentment. He did not want sympathy."

Paul's independence is genuine, but, as we expected, its main manifestation—the affair with Miriam—is abortive. If one of the marks of tragedy is an awareness of the reality of insoluble questions, then

Lawrence's delineation of this relationship, particularly in its last phase, has something of tragic intensity. We see vividly how, given these people in this background, only this result could ensue. The dark and ineluctable fate in whose toils the lovers are trapped is their own history and nature—character is destiny. The degree of individual responsibility for what, when it happens, is seen to be inevitable is clearly presented, yet in no spirit of censorious fault-finding. There is a wholly unsentimental tenderness in the scene of Miriam and Paul living together as man and wife for a few brief hours, each sensing how precious these hours are and almost destroying them through over-concern. And the irridescent near-symbolism of Paul eating cherries on the tree, while Miriam stands below, by the skeletons of four dead birds and bleached cherry stones "picked clear of flesh" is, we now recognize peculiarly Lawrentian, recalling such earlier scenes as Mrs. Morel among the moonlit lilies, the 'swing' scene in chapter VIII and, in this chapter, Paul's vivid awareness of the irises and his chewing the flower as he tells his mother of his intention to break with Miriam.

The title of the chapter "The Test on Miriam" may be intended to suggest that it is to be seen primarily from this point of view, as a challenge which in some way, Miriam failed. Certainly, Miriam is no more sentimentalized than any of the other characters. Her over-anxiety to possess Paul's 'soul' and her pathetic resolve to make of her body a sacrifice to her love, however distasteful the effort may be, are presented with sympathy but without indulgence. The chapter ends on a note of haunting casualness: " 'Well, leave her alone,' " replied his mother.

"So he left her, and she was alone. Very few people cared for her, and she for very few people. She remained alone with herself, waiting."

But the test, as we see, is not for Miriam alone. In one way or another it is a test for all the principal characters involved, not forgetting Clara Dawes, with whom "his brow cleared, and he was gay again". Again, we are given an insight into Paul's relationship with Clara that goes beyond that of Paul himself: "But insidiously, without his knowing it the warmth he felt for Clara drew him away from Miriam, for whom he felt responsible, and to whom he felt he belonged."

This chapter dramatizes Paul's struggle to escape the responsibility and end the sense of belonging, and the price paid, not only by himself but by the others involved, to achieve these ends. It also shows us a

Paul who is on his way towards severing the umbilical cord of his mother's possessive love. He is, at least temporarily, 'free'. What does he do with this hard-won and precariously held freedom?

Chapter Twelve

On a cynical view we might say that he rushes straight out of one kind of bondage into another, out of Miriam's arms and into Clara's. And there is some truth in this. The next phase of Paul's behaviour is fairly predictable. But the predictability is only a measure of the author's success in enabling us to see his hero from outside as well as from within. And it is never a total predictability, which would be tedious and unilluminating. We can foresee the broad outline of Paul's growth, but its details have that mingling of surprise and inevitability in retrospect which the great novelists give us.

The stark title of the chapter is an accurate enough indication of its main concern. It tells us how Paul Morel finds, in and through Clara, that union of physical and emotional fulfilment which he was unable to achieve with Miriam. We should now be able to recognize that it is characteristic of Lawrence to begin a chapter dealing mainly with Paul's emotional life with a paragraph summarizing his economic success as an artist. He is doing well, selling designs, paintings and so on. But this paragraph does more than tell us this. His preference for painting "large figures, full of light . . . rather definite figures that had a certain luminous quality, like some of Michaelangelo's people", gives a hint of what he is looking for in life itself, a quality which he believes he has found in Clara Dawes. And we see too the first clear awareness in Paul of his true vocation.

"He was twenty-four when he said his first confident thing to his mother.

"'Mother', he said, 'I'll make a painter that they'll attend to.'" But it is fair to say that Paul's art does not seem to matter very deeply to him. He is frustrated at all three possible points of outward growth— his work, his painting, and his women. And, in spite of the fact that the young Lawrence was a keen amateur painter, it is curious how little is made in the novel of the details of the art.

That Clara's attraction for Paul is overwhelmingly physical hardly needs elaborating. From the moment, at the beginning of the chapter when he touches her while drawing her dress tighter across her body ("He had touched her. His whole body was quivering with the sensation") till the climax where he embraces her naked in the firelight, his excited sense of her bodily presence is as palpable as a taste on the tongue. It is exactly what we missed even in the most intimate love scenes with Miriam. What is worth noting is that no moral judgment is enforced on us with regard to this fact. Or rather, no simple moral condemnation on the one hand or sentimental identification on the other. Such judgment as we do make is delicate, tentative and sympathetic, a heightening of our total awareness rather than a rigid endorsement of this or that dogma.

There is inevitably a certain degree of sympathy for the hero in any novel, if only because we see so many things through his eyes (though not necessarily *only* through his eyes). But such sympathy is here qualified in several ways. To begin with, there is the sense I have already noted, of an almost automatic reaction in Paul, a kind of 'rebound' from Miriam to Clara. Allied to this are the indications that in Paul's infatuation (the word chooses itself) with Clara there is, paradoxically, less, rather than more of himself than there was in the strained relationship with Miriam. The terms in which his initial anxiety is presented suggest a precarious control as well as an absence of the whole self. The division between his ordinary life and his moments with her is sharper than it ever was with Miriam. The one does not irradiate the other, as we might expect if the kind of fulfilment Paul seeks really had been achieved. Rather the two halves remain distinct and unconnected: "Again came over him the feeling that he would lose consciousness. He set his teeth and went upstairs. He had done everything correctly yet, and he would do so. In the morning things seemed a long way off, as they do to a man under chloroform. He himself seemed under a tight band of constraint. Then there was his other self, in the distance, doing things, entering stuff in a ledger, and he watched that far-off him carefully to see he made no mistake."

Most important in preventing us from identifying ourselves wholly with Paul Morel at this stage are the various viewpoints of the other characters involved, directly or marginally in the new relationship. The variety and objectivity which, in various degrees, they provide play an indispensable part in saving this part of the novel from sentimentality.

Chief of these characters is Clara herself. While the experience is as vital to her as it is to Paul, we are made sharply aware that its meaning and quality are different, because of her particular history and temperament. We are explicitly reminded that she is five or six years older than Paul—"'What does it matter?'" exclaims Paul. But we see that to her it *does* matter, as it matters that she is a married woman, as it matters, indeed, that she is a woman, living in a society where the limits of feminine freedom are fairly clearly marked. To Paul, it is the first rapture of physical awakening. To Clara it is a more ambiguous experience, holding in it the threat of disillusion as much as the promise of fulfilment. "Quiet and uncomfortable", and "resigned" are the words used here to describe Clara's feelings. And an awareness of her attitude modifies our response to Paul's.

Other cross-lights which light up the scene for us are the comments of the two mothers. Mrs. Morel, as we have already seen, does not fear Clara as she feared Miriam. "Mrs. Morel measured herself against the younger woman, and found herself easily stronger." Her confidence is, we feel, justified, even though "Paul watching, felt his heart contract with pain. His mother looked so small, and sallow, and done-for beside the luxuriant Clara." (Or perhaps because of this. Even in the midst of his bliss with Clara, Paul feels more sharply the anguish of his mother's ageing.) But Mrs. Morel's final comment on Clara is: "'But you'll tire of her, my son; *you know you will*'" (my italics). By now, we know that the mother knows her son well enough for this judgment to be more than wishful thinking. It is something that, at the deepest level, the son himself recognizes.

More explicitly hostile is the reaction of Clara's mother when Clara takes Paul home from the theatre to spend the night at their house. Her main concern is, naturally enough, with the social aspects of the situation, the propriety of the clothes the young people are wearing, and the anxiety to see that they sleep in separate beds. Paul has no great difficulty in winning the verbal battle between them, but the old woman is not entirely annihilated. We certainly see something comical in the hatred Paul feels for her because she won't go to bed until her daughter does; and to that extent she too helps us to keep our distance from Paul.

Miriam is yet another character through whom this phase of Paul's life is presented to us. It is one of Lawrence's finest strokes to show us through Miriam's eyes the scene in which Clara and Paul are enjoying themselves in the garden after tea. "At that moment Miriam was entering through the garden door. She saw Clara go up to him, saw him turn, and saw them come to rest together. Something in their perfect isolation together made her know that it was accomplished between them, that they were, as she put it, married. She walked very slowly down the cinder-track of the long garden." In a sense Miriam is here made to endorse Paul's own valuation of the affair. But the nervous, edgy tone of the dialogue which immediately follows carries its own implicit comment. However perfect their isolation together may be, there is something lacking in the new relationship, a lack which Paul betrays in his falsification of what Miriam had meant to him ("'There never *was* a great deal more than talk between us'") and his resentment over Mrs. Morel and Clara discussing Miriam. The final effect of Miriam's perception is, paradoxically, to alert us to the possibility that she is mistaken.

But when all this has been said, it seems to me that the dominant note of this chapter is one of freedom, spontaneity and relaxation, in Lawrence's own word, of gaiety. There is a sharp contrast with the intense yet somehow constricted atmosphere of the later stages of the Miriam affair. As we see the lovers hesitantly holding hands at the cinema or walking arm in arm by the muddy river bank on a rainy afternoon or resplendent at the theatre, we are aware in them, beyond all the tensions and reservations, of a quality of joy which is surely one of the Lawrentian values we can all respond to. It is not a quality that can easily be illustrated by quotation since its impact is pervasive rather than local, but perhaps it can be seen in an explicit and fairly compressed form in the episode of the old woman at whose house the lovers stop for tea. "The old lady at whose house they had tea was roused into gaiety by them." And when Clara says "'If she knew'", Paul's reply catches, at least in part, our own response: "'Well, she doesn't know; and it shows we're nice in ourselves, at any rate. You look quiet enough to satisfy an archangel, and I'm sure I feel harmless—so—if it makes you look nice, and makes folk happy when they have us, and makes us happy—why, we're not cheating them out of much!'"

This is not of course, the whole story, nor are we asked to accept it as such. But we can respond to it and still keep an open mind as to the soundness or otherwise of Paul's whole position. And this, I think, is what the novel invites us to do.

Chapter Thirteen

This chapter is somewhat misleadingly titled, for though Baxter Dawes appears in the two principal incidents in it, we are hardly invited to take an independent interest in him or his point of view. This is not to say that his portrayal is unconvincing or inadequate. It is perfectly convincing and adequate within its limits; these limits are suggested broadly speaking, by saying that Baxter serves both as a contrast to Paul Morel and a means of making us more fully aware of Clara's character and attitude.

The brief opening scene where Baxter taunts Paul about his visit to the theatre is very sharply realized, mainly in terms of the racy dialogue (not quite dialect, yet related to it) at which Lawrence was so skilful. It suggests the social milieu and catches exactly the sharp edges of male malice and envy beneath the brittle bonhomie. Its inconclusiveness as an incident also prepares us for the scene later on where Baxter Dawes lies in wait for Paul one evening and beats him unconscious.

We may feel that in this scene Dawes gets a raw deal, especially from the barmaid (after all, the superior lecturing tone of Paul's remarks on the aristocracy is aggravating enough, even if Dawes didn't have the personal grievance that he does). But in the chapter as a whole he certainly does not appear in an entirely unsympathetic light. At least as a lover, Clara almost prefers him to Paul: "'You can't come out of yourself, you can't,'" she tells him, "'Baxter could do that better than you.'" And a revealing detail which occurs immediately after Baxter has knocked Paul unconscious may suggest that the former is not altogether the unfeeling lout that almost everyone takes him to be: ". . . dimly in his consciousness as he went, he felt on his foot the place where his boot had knocked against one of the lad's bones. The knock seemed to re-echo inside him; he hurried to get away from it." Baxter's confident physical prowess is also contrasted with Paul's awkwardness, underlining a sense in which the hero of this novel is *not* a conventional hero at all.

In a fairly obvious sense both these incidents are, in their context, ironical. For they both show the 'hero' put in a situation where he is called upon to defend his 'lady' when the real truth is, as we see, that she no longer *is* his 'lady' in any important sense. It is true that this chapter, even more than the last, shows us the culmination of the love between Clara and Paul. But it is a culmination that has anxiety and uncertainty as its prelude—"Clara looked at her lover closely. There was something in him she hated, a sort of detached criticism of herself, a coldness which made her woman's soul harden against him"—and which topples over almost immediately into dissolution. "Clara was, indeed, passionately in love with him, and he with her, as far as passion went." The qualifying phrase hints at the inadequacy; with Clara Paul finds the 'passion' he missed with Miriam, but still there is something lacking. The scene where the two lovers lie on the grass with the peewits calling overhead is beautifully rendered, but part of its impact comes from our awareness that it is a tremulous moment of bliss, precariously achieved and in its nature ephemeral. Neither of the lovers can see it as anything other than a unique exception: "But Clara was not satisfied. Something great was there, she knew; something great enveloped her. But it did not keep her. In the morning it was not the same. They had *known*, but she could not keep the moment." And her pathetic efforts to cling to Paul have the inevitable effect of driving him further away from her (for had not Miriam too repelled him by her excessive possessiveness?) until he spends his time with her almost out of pity. As for Paul, after the climactic experience, "In the morning he had considerable peace, and was happy in himself. It seemed almost as if he had known the baptism of fire in passion, and it left him at rest. But it was not Clara. It was something that happened because of her, but it was not her."

It seems as if this relationship too is to founder, just like the one with Miriam. What prevents it from being a mere repetition, with minor variations, of the earlier affair is very largely Paul's reaction to what is happening. For he is no longer so ready to rationalize his failure and look for explanations in other people. He is beginning to suspect that he may be responsible for more of the frustration than he had realized. The element of self-extenuation in his remark to his mother "'She's fearfully in love with me, but it's not very deep'", is immediately scotched by his mother's reply: "'But quite as deep as your feeling for her'", with which Paul is constrained to agree; it prompts the further reflection that he is "wronging" his "women" in some way which he is as yet unable to define. And the author comments: "He went on painting rather despairingly; he had touched the quick of the trouble."

As his awareness of himself grows, his relationship to his mother alters. The process we have already seen is intensified and accelerated: "There

was now a good deal of his life of which necessarily he could not speak
to his mother. He had a life apart from her—his sexual life. The rest she
still kept. But he felt he had to conceal something from her, and it irked
him. There was a certain silence between them, and he felt he had, in
that silence, to defend himself against her; he felt condemned by her.
Then sometimes he hated her, and pulled at her bondage. His life wanted
to free itself of her. . . . At this period, unknowingly, he resisted his
mother's influence."

I have omitted a few sentences which make this paragraph an even
more explicit intrusion of the author into the story (that "unknowingly"
in the last sentence is obviously Lawrence's, not Paul Morel's). As I
have already indicated, I think this sort of authorial summary is not only
acceptable but necessary for the kind of novel Lawrence is writing;
we must have a *reliable* account of Paul's development at various crucial
stages if we are to sense the discrepancy between Paul's own view and the
truth. In this case, our knowledge that he is resisting his mother's
influence gives an added poignancy to the final scenes of this chapter,
those dealing with the crisis in the mother's illness. The sheer intensity
of presentation of these scenes is heightened rather than diminished by
the matter-of-fact details (doctors' fees, train schedules, and the like)
which surround them; it also shows up the love scenes with Clara as
lukewarm in comparison. This is not an adverse criticism, since the hold
which the mother has on the son even when he is drawing away from
her is precisely the novelist's point. Once again, quotation cannot deal
justly with the scenes, for their power is cumulative. But a tiny detail
like this, which could easily have lapsed into sentimentality, rings
absolutely true: "Her eyes were so blue—such a wonderful forget-me-
not blue! He felt if only they had been of a different colour he could
have borne it better." And surely this must be one of the most touching
examples of the 'objective correlative' of grief in modern English fiction:
"He sat in the kitchen, smoking. Then he tried to brush some grey ash
off his coat. He looked again. It was one of his mother's grey hairs.
It was so long! He held it up, and it drifted into the chimney. He let go.
The long grey hair floated and was gone in the blackness of the chimney." Again, it is because Lawrence, as one critic has said "is never afraid
to give himself away by writing badly", that he can achieve this kind of
effect: "He cried, he did not know why. It was his blood weeping."

In these scenes the ageing father makes one of his brief and infrequent
appearances and is utterly convincing in his awkward tenderness; scenes

such as these confirm me in my view that the treatment of the elder Morel is more sympathetic than is generally allowed. While our main angle of vision on Mrs. Morel's illness is of course, Paul, it is by no means the only one. In addition to Morel's genuine and barely articulate grief, there is that of the rest of the family ("under the blue sky they could all see she was dying"), the impersonal sympathy of the doctors and the brief but vivid perspective of the chorus of neighbours ("And they all saw death on her face, they said. It was a great event in the street."). Thus, while enabling us fully to share the intensity of Paul's reaction to his mother's illness, Lawrence is careful to set the event in a perspective wider than the protagonist's alone.

Chapter Fourteen

Both the main narrative lines—the Clara–Paul–Baxter Dawes triangle and the story of the relationship between Mrs. Morel and her son, come to a head simultaneously. We also see the last forlorn flicker of the love affair with Miriam. The handling of the former is a good example of how a great novelist can take the tiredest and most cliché-ridden raw material, such as the rivalry of two men for the same woman, and explore it in a way which offers new insight into human conduct and its motives. Lawrence clearly refuses to tap the simple black-and-white antitheses which the situation offers—brute strength (Dawes) *vs.* intellect (Morel), the horny-handed worker versus the sensitive artist, the gentleman versus the boor, and so forth. The relationship as it is presented to us certainly includes elements of all these, but is too subtle and intricate to be pinned down to any.

The way in which the relationship between the two men is worked out for instance is unexpected, but it would be incredible only if we had not given due weight to earlier indications that Dawes is not simply an unmitigated villain. He grows in stature here but not in a widly impossible direction. His hostility to Paul, his taciturnity and introspectiveness are transformed rather than abolished. Thus, while Paul and Baxter Dawes achieve a mutual respect for each other, the quite real dislike between the two is always present beneath the surface, ready to erupt not only in the explicit comment ("Then they did not talk any more. The instinct to murder each other had returned. They almost avoided each other") but in the strained rhythms of the dialogue. An extended quotation is needed to bring this out. "'And I don't see' said Paul, 'why you shouldn't go on where you left off.'

"'What——,' said Dawes, suggestively.

"'Yes—fit your old home together again.'

"Dawes hid his face and shook his head.

"'Couldn't be done,' he said, and looked up with an ironic smile.

"'Why? Because you don't want?'

"'Perhaps.'

"They smoked in silence. Dawes showed his teeth as he bit his pipe stem.

"'You mean you don't want her?' asked Paul.

"Dawes stared up at the picture with a caustic expression on his face.

"'I hardly know,' he said.

"The smoke floated softly up.

"'I believe she wants you,' said Paul.

"'Do you?' replied the other, soft, satirical, abstract."

The growing understanding between the two men precipitates a result for which we have already been prepared—the severing of the last links between Paul and Clara and the reunion between Clara and her husband. While Clara is becoming increasingly critical of Paul it is difficult not to feel in these episodes that the author is concerned to 'protect' Paul in a special way. It is not merely that the turn of events could not have been more convenient from Paul's point of view; just when he finds the girl irksome, she herself turns against him and rejoins a husband with whom, we had been earlier led to believe, she has found life quite impossible. What worries us is Lawrence's seeming unawareness of the degree of self-concern in Paul's efforts to reconcile Clara with her husband. There is more identification than detachment in this comment on Paul's feelings: "He only wanted to be left alone now. He had his own trouble, which was almost too much to bear. Clara only tormented him and made him tired. He was not sorry when he left her." And the note of justification for Paul is unmistakable here, with its suggestion that, when all is said and done, it is Clara, and she alone, who is deluded: "Yet Clara realized that Morel was withdrawing from the circle, leaving her the option to stay with her husband. It angered her. He was a mean fellow, after all, to take what he wanted and then give her back. She did not remember that she herself had what she wanted, and really, at the bottom of her heart, wished to be given back."

Elsewhere though, and most notably in the scenes describing Paul's feelings immediately before and after losing his mother, Lawrence preserves a fine balance between clinical detachment from and complete identification with his protagonist. It is significant that Paul does not tell his mother of his interview with Baxter Dawes—not so much that he is confident in himself as that his relationship with his mother has worsened considerably. Perhaps unconsciously he feels some vague responsibility for her illness. We may recall Annie's words, "'She's been having these pains for months at home and nobody looking after her,'" and, when Paul says his mother never told him she was unwell, "'If I'd been at home,' said Annie 'I should have seen for myself.'" Whether or not it is this feeling of guilt which turns to fear, there is no doubt that fear is the keynote of the changed relationship between mother and son: "Paul and she were afraid of each other. He knew, and she knew, that she was dying. But they kept up a pretence of cheerfulness." But the cost of this pretence is very high indeed and at last it becomes intolerable. There is a terrible little scene describing Paul and Clara making love after he had come from watching at his mother's sick-bed, a scene, moreover, which we realize is far from being unique: "'Take me!' he said simply.

"Occasionally she would. But she was afraid. When he had her then, there was something in it that made her shrink away from him—something unnatural. She grew to dread him. He was so quiet, yet so strange. She was afraid of the man who was not there with her, whom she could feel behind this make-believe cover; somebody sinister, that filled her with horror."

Reading passages such as these, we understand one of the senses in which Lawrence is a religious writer; he apprehended sexual fulfilment so deeply as a sacramental act, that when it is less than a total commitment on the part of both parties involved, it can only be an act of blasphemy against 'the deed of life'.

The toll which the guilt-fear feelings engendered by his mother's illness exacts from Paul shows itself not only, as above, in the poisoning of his relations with Clara, but more generally in a weakening hold on the physical world. "Things seemed as if they did not exist." This is the first stage of what later becomes a sort of death-wish on Paul's part ("It was almost as if he were agreeing to die also"). The tangle of emotions and sensations in which Paul is enmeshed—weariness, hope-

lessness, possessive love—is beautifully caught in the rhythm of lines
such as these: "And he sat by the bedside, slowly, rhythmically stroking
her brows with his finger-tips, stroking her eyes shut, soothing her,
holding her fingers in his free hand. They could hear the sleepers'
breathing in the other rooms."

The single paragraph describing Miriam's futile efforts to console
Paul which comes almost immediately after this provides an anguished
contrast ("And she thought she had soothed him and done him good").

These scenes which dramatize the last agonized weeks of Mrs.
Morel's life are among the most powerful in the whole novel. While
they are full of resonance and implication, we are constantly aware that
it is a real woman who is dying, and dying in a particularly painful and
ugly way; Paul may be wrapped up in his own reaction to the dying, but
Lawrence isn't. By widening his focus to involve both Annie and old
Morel he objectifies the victim's agony for us—and once again the
rhythm of the words is as evocative as their sense. "Again came the
great snoring breath. Again they hung suspended. Again it was given
back, long and harsh. The sound, so irregular, at such wide intervals,
sounded through the house. Morel, in his room, slept on. Paul and Annie
sat crouched, huddled, motionless. The great snoring sound began
again—there was a painful pause while the breath was held—back came
the rasping breath." And even more poignantly, the scene of crisis
within is contrasted, through Paul's senses, with the ordinary, un-
emphatic routine of daily living in the world outside: "And in a few
minutes Paul heard his father's heavy steps go thudding over the deaden-
ing snow. Miners called in the street as they tramped in gangs to work.
The terrible, long-drawn breaths continued—heave—heave—heave;
then a long pause—then—ah-h-h-h-h! as it came back. Far away over
the snow sounded the hooters of the ironworks."

If we insist, we can perhaps extract some kind of 'symbolic' significance
from the fact that Paul is directly responsible for the death of his mother,
since he gives her an overdose of morphia (*he* must take the initiative,
he must kill his mother before he can be a man, etc.), but the scene
itself at any rate impresses us first and foremost with its realistic power.
The realism is, like all realism that is also art, selective. We have for
instance, the haunting detail of the daughter and son after thay have
decided to put the morphia in the mother's drink—"Then they both
laughed together like two conspiring children." And, to make clear that
this is not simply to add a macabre touch for its own sake, the author's

comment: "On top of all their horror flicked this little sanity." The repeated description of the mother as a child which runs like a refrain throughout the actual scene of the poisoning is the only direct comment. It contains at least a triple charge of irony. First, the simple reversal of roles (mother = child, child = 'mother', i.e.—nourisher). Then, our realization that this 'nourishment' is poison, this 'mother' a killer. And finally, our further awareness that, in so far as this killing is a deed of kindness, it is truly a 'motherly' act. For the rest, the dramatic ironies implicit in the ensuing dialogue (due to our knowing what the mother does not) are left to make their own impact.

When the death comes, we are left in no doubt that it is, at least in part, a blessing. The chapter is, after all, titled "The Release". But there is more than one kind of release. There is the release of the prisoner from the cell, but there is also the release of the bullet from the gun. Paul is not only liberated by his mother's death from an emotional stranglehold, he is also hurled into life with the worst possible equipment—an inadequate grip on reality: "It made him ashamed. So, secretly ashamed because he was in such a mess, because his own hold on life was so unsure because nobody held him, feeling unsubstantial, shadowy, as if he did not count for much in this concrete world, he drew himself together smaller and smaller."

It seems an insoluble dilemma, because Paul's 'hold on life' depended on his mother's 'hold' on him—and the entire novel has shown us the disastrous results of *that* hold.

Chapter Fifteen

The last brief chapter dramatically renders the depth and extent of the shadowiness and insubstantiality to which Paul's life has shrunk after his mother's death. The chapter moves from a brief general survey of Paul's life to concentrate all the accumulated sense of emptiness, frustration and torment of that life in a single climactic scene involving a ghost from the not quite dead past, Miriam. That Paul is no longer able to paint is a disturbing reminder that he owed his creative strength in part to his mother's 'hold' on him, as well as his less favourable attributes. His apprehension of the outer world has weakened so much that the scenes describing his aimless wanderings take on a somnambulistic rhythm:

"Everything seemed so different, so unreal. There seemed no reason why people should go along the street, and houses pile up in the daylight. There seemed no reason why these things should occupy the space, instead of leaving it empty. His friends talked to him; he heard the sounds and he answered. But why there should be the noise of speech he could not understand."

Sounds, sights, sensations, all lose definition and significance in the paralysed consciousness of the hero. The bustling energy of the tramcars is as devoid of significance as the first thrust of the snowdrops through an element which has simply sunk into the blurred unreality of "the grey". And conversely, the apparently banal or trivial can leap into life and meaning if it sparks a connection with the lost source of Paul's energy:

"Suddenly a piece of paper started near his feet and blew down the pavement. He stood still, rigid, with clenched fists, a flame of agony going over him. And he saw again the sickroom, his mother, her eyes. Unconsciously he had been with her, in her company. The swift hop of the paper reminded him she was gone. But he had been with her. He wanted everything to stand still so that he could be with her again."

His mental dialogues with himself are, as we expect, not only inconclusive but serve to heighten his agony by bringing it into an intense focus of consciousness. Only a blind determination that "he would not own that life had beaten him, or that death had beaten him" keeps him going, but not for long, for he has nowhere to go. In his extremity he turns to Miriam but the manner in which he turns to her makes it almost a foregone conclusion that she cannot sustain him. "In despair he thought of Miriam. Perhaps—perhaps?"

We have a strong sense of *déja vù* on encountering this scene. The difference is that Paul's mother is now dead, but, like Caesar, she is much more powerfully present in death than in life. We feel her unseen dominance over Paul in every line of the taut, uneasy dialogue in this long scene. And we are not alone, for Miriam feels it too, as her stumbling reply to Paul's question makes clear:

"'And if we married?' he asked.

"'At any rate, I could prevent you wasting yourself and being a prey to other women—like—like Clara.'"

Nothing is less surprising than the outcome of this last interview.

We are given a brief but vivid glimpse of Miriam's future—she too, will be one of the 'new' women, economically independent, finding as much satisfaction as she can in her career for a thwarted emotional life. And though part of the blame for the failure is laid on Miriam's shrinking from the physical aspects of sex, we are left in no doubt that failure is inherent in the situation, for Paul is making contradictory demands. He wants to regain and retain his individuality, yet he also wants her to "take him and relieve him of the responsibility of himself". He is looking in short, for the lost world of his mother's love where "Joy and authority" were both present, where he could be son and lover both.

We see that Miriam is deluded in her pathetic belief that he would somehow return to her. Author and hero unite to impart an unmistakable air of finality to the summing up of this beautiful, troubled and hopeless affair: "He felt, in leaving her, he was defrauding her of life. But he knew that in staying, stifling the inner desperate man, he was denying his own life. And he did not hope to give life to her by denying his own."

The ending of the book is as irreducibly ambiguous as its central relationship. Against the overwhelming sense of loss and uprootedness suffered by Paul is counterposed his obstinate will not only to survive but to find a new source of growth and fulfilment. The closing cadences of the book have a purposive tread about them, matching the hero's resolution: "But no, he would not give in. Turning sharply, he walked towards the city's gold phosphorescence. His fists were shut, his mouth set fast. He would not take that direction, to the darkness, to follow her. He walked towards the faintly humming, glowing town, quickly." But remembering that for Paul now, "the realest thing was the thick darkness at night", we may perhaps wonder how significant in the total pattern of the book this gesture of freedom is, what resources he has for coping with reality if he really turns away from the one relationship which, as far as we have seen, gave meaning and purpose to his existence. Perhaps Lawrence was not so wide off the mark as his critics have tried to make out when, in the celebrated letter to Edward Garnett about *Sons and Lovers*, he described his hero as left at the end of the novel "with the drift towards death".

Conclusion

Sons and Lovers was written over fifty years ago and in some ways it bears the mark of its time and place. It is a novel of the English Midlands, a region whose way of life is significantly different from that of the south; its religious background is dissent and its political tradition radical. It is a community with its own fiercely independent outlook, and one whose free spirits—Clara Dawes, Miriam Leivers, Paul Morel—strive to achieve intellectual and social identity without any cultural centre from which to take their bearings. Thus, while 'individualism' wears a more heroic aspect in this kind of community, its tragic possibilities lie closer to the surface of life, as the end of the novel makes us realize.

As we are aware of a particular mode of life in a particular community, so too, we have the sense of a given moment of history. *Sons and Lovers* begins at a time when industrialism still lived more or less at ease with the older rural order. The paternalism and geniality which surrounds Mr. Jordan's surgical appliance factory (with Mr. Jordan himself a working manager rather than an absentee shareholder) belong to an earlier and more human stage of the industrial-economic process than the factory where Arthur Seaton is determined not to let the bastards grind you down (*Saturday Night and Sunday Morning*). And a figure like Clara is typical of the many militant suffragettes of the early years of this century.

But in many important respects *Sons and Lovers* strikes us as vividly contemporary. Harry T. Moore has called it 'the last nineteenth-century novel'. I think the truer comment is Frank O'Connor's, namely that it begins as a nineteenth-century novel and ends as a modern one. We can almost plot the change through the changing chapter titles, from "The Early Married Life of the Morels" to "Derelict". One aspect of this 'modernity' is the candour with which sexual relationships are treated. (The archetypal nature of the mother–son relationship depicted in the book is attested not only by the findings of psychoanalysis but also by the innumerable novels of the past fifty years which have dealt explicitly with the same basic situation.) More significantly, the novel is typical of much contemporary literature in having a crippled hero, one who is victim rather than agent. And such a hero's view of the world is appropriately presented not through the orderly chronological sequences of most nineteenth-century fiction, but through a freer and more introspective form, where the emphasis is constantly on the emotional predicament of the protagonists. Finally, the novel is modern in being entirely free from moral didacticism. In an essay written towards the end of his life, Lawrence drew what might appear to be one of the 'morals' of Sons and Lovers:

"My mother spoilt her life with her moral frenzy against John Barleycorn. To be sure she had occasion to detest the alcoholic stuff. But why the moral frenzy? It made a tragedy out of what was only a nuisance. And at fifty, when the best part of life was gone, she realized it. And then what would she not have given to have her life again, her young children, her tipsy husband, and a proper natural insouciance, to get the best out of it all. When woman tries to be too much mistress of fate, particularly of other people's fates, what a tragedy!"

(Women are so Cocksure)

But even as we assent to this as a summary judgment, we realize how much more compassionate and comprehensive the novelist's vision is than the essayist's.

In the fifty odd years since its publication, Sons and Lovers has attracted more attention—biographical, psychoanalytical and critical—than almost any other English novel of the twentieth century, with the possible exception of Ulysses. We are far enough away from the circumstances of its original publication not to become entangled in the futile question of whether or not Lawrence was 'unfair' to the real-life counterparts of his characters. We understand and sympathize with the real-life 'Miriam's' chagrin over the novel, and if we wish we may read her own moving record of the same tract of experience (a book well worth reading for its own sake). But it is mere naïveté or worse to insist on judging Sons and Lovers from Miriam's viewpoint; one might as well judge the first part of Henry VI. from the standpoint of the historical Joan of Arc.

Closely related to the biographical commentary is the psychoanalytical interpretation. While this occasionally leads to valuable insights, too often it tends to divert attention from what is actually present and realized in the novel to its problematic psychoanalytical

'meaning' and the novel degenerates into a code which has to be cracked.
Also the characters are in danger of being flattened into rigidly determined puppets and small details are distorted or inflated out of all
proportion because they are important in the hypothetical analytical
scheme. Thus a recent critic tells us' that Gertrude Morel "'gives'
William's girls to Walter Morel by purposely confusing the father and
son." If the reader troubles to refer to the context (Ch. III) he will see
that the epithet 'purposely' is quite unwarranted. But it is necessary for
the critic's point about "a chiasmus of 'giving' on the parts of the women
in the novel".[1]

Sons and Lovers has certainly not lacked strictly literary-critical
attention, especially in the last few years. But much of this has tended to
see the book chiefly as a precursor of the later Lawrence. I have no wish
to deny that both The Rainbow and Women in Love are greater novels
than Sons and Lovers, nor that the earlier novel often illuminates the
later ones. But my own concern has been to show in what way Sons and
Lovers is an enjoyable and important novel in its own right.

To this end, my commentary has been for the most part an attempt
to record faithfully the actual experience of reading the novel rather
than a pondered retrospective judgment on it. With a novel like Sons
and Lovers, where we are invited to share in a developing experience
more or less localized in a single consciousness, this seems to me an
appropriate way to get at the questions: "What kind of work is this?
What exactly is going on here?" As for the other pair of questions:
"How good is this work and why?" I hope my emphasis on the part
played by point of view in controlling our response will go some way
towards suggesting an answer, while also acting as a corrective to the
tendency to assume that the novel was written by Paul Morel. I have
also tried by implication to refute the charges sometimes made that the
novel is 'broken-backed' in that the first part and the second are insuffi-
ciently related, and that it is needlessly repetitive. The detailed comments
are intended to show how the destiny of the son is rooted in the fate of
the father, and how the dead son's history is not a mere rehearsal of the
living one's, but a prelude to its understanding. If a more general
statement of the value of Sons and Lovers is needed, I can think of none
better than D. H. Lawrence's own words in Lady Chatterly's Lover (IX):

'And here lies the vast importance of the novel, properly handled.
It can inform and lead into new places the flow of our sympathetic

[1] Daniel A. Weiss, Oedipus in Nottingham: D. H. Lawrence

consciousness, and can lead our sympathy away in recoil from things gone dead.'

'I tell you I have written a great book. . . . Read my novel, it is a great novel,' Lawrence wrote to Edward Garnett. Even if the adjective had not been worn hopelessly threadbare, I see no reason to quarrel with Lawrence's verdict.

A Note on the Text

Lawrence began writing *Sons and Lovers* (originally entitled *Paul Morel*) in the latter part of 1910. The novel was published in 1913.

As already mentioned, the real-life Miriam (Mrs. John R. Wood, *née* Jessie Chambers) has given her own version of the events and relationships depicted in the novel (*D. H. Lawrence: A Personal Record*, 1935). In addition, however, Lawrence showed parts of the manuscript while he was writing it to Jessie Chambers. She made many corrections and also wrote some episodes which Lawrence incorporated in the final version. For full details, see *D. H. Lawrence: His Life and Works* by Harry T. Moore.

In the final stages, Lawrence also had some help from his wife, Frieda. More important is the editing of the final manuscript by Edward Garnett, then reader for Duckworth, who published the novel. Garnett's editorial deletions range from a few lines to several pages. For further details see *Sons and Lovers: Sources and Criticism*, edited by E. W. Tedlock, Jr.

In 1963, the manuscript of the final version of *Sons and Lovers* was bought by the Library of the University of California at Berkeley from the estate of the American psychoanalyst, A. A. Brill. Two parts of an earlier version (*Paul Morel*) are in the Humanities Research Centre of the University of Texas.

Further Reading

Of the making of books on Lawrence there is apparently no end. The following Bibliography is more select than most. The fullest catalogue of Lawrence's writings (together with a select listing of criticism) is by Warren Roberts, in the Soho Bibliographies series.

The definitive life of D. H. Lawrence is Edward Nehls' monumental three-volume composite biography (1957-9). More compact but very thorough studies are two by Harry T. Moore, *The Life and Works of D. H. Lawrence* (1951), and *The Intelligent Heart: The Story of D. H. Lawrence* (1954; reissued in 1974 as *The Priest of Love*). In addition to the memoir by Jessie Chambers, *Young Lorenzo: The Early Life of D. H. Lawrence* (1932), by Lawrence's sister Ada (in collaboration with Stuart Gelder), and *D. H. Lawrence's Princess* (1951), by Helen Corke cover the period dealt with in the novel.

Among critical studies, *The Dark Sun* by Graham Hough (1956), *The Deed of Life* (1963), by Julian Moynihan and *D. H. Lawrence* (1964), by R. P. Draper are all readable and straightforward introductory surveys. Mark Spilka's *The Love Ethic of D. H. Lawrence* (1955), is particularly good on the flower-symbolism in *Sons and Lovers*. F. R. Leavis' influential study *D. H. Lawrence: Novelist* (1955), does not deal at length with *Sons and Lovers*.

For those interested in the psychoanalytic aspects of the novel, one of the earliest and still one of the least eccentric studies is 'A Freudian Appreciation' by Alfred Booth Kuttner (*The Psychoanalytic Review*, III, 3, July 1913). More elaborate and sometimes illuminating is *Oedipus in Nottingham* (1962), by Daniel A. Weiss. See also 'Lawrence's Quarrel with Freud', *Freudianism and the Literary Mind* by Frederick J. Hoffman (1957), and *Love against Hate* by Karl Menninger (1942).

David Daiches' *The Novel and the Modern World* (revised edition, 1960), and Frank O'Connor's *The Mirror in the Roadway* (1955), contain useful discussions of the novel, as does Dorothy Van Ghent's *The English Novel: Form and Function* (1953). Stimulating studies of *Sons and Lovers* are Mark Schorer's 'Technique as Discovery' (*Hudson Review*, I, i, 1948—frequently reprinted in American critical anthologies), Seymour Betsky's essay in *The Achievement of D. H. Lawrence* (1953), edited by Frederick J. Hoffman and Harry T. Moore, and 'The Unattainable Self' by Louis Fraiberg in *Twelve Original Essays on Great English Novels* (1960), edited by Charles Shapiro. Alfred Kazin's introduction to the Modern Library edition (1962) is also well worth reading. Other useful studies are those by Keith Sagar in *The Art of D. H. Lawrence* (1966) and Barbara Hardy in *The Appropriate Form* (1964) which takes issue with Mark Schorer's essay.

Many of Lawrence's own writings are particularly relevant to *Sons and Lovers*. Among these are the celebrated letter to Edward Garnett, dated November 4th, 1912, several poems of the period and the two essays 'Women are so Cocksure' and 'Nottingham and the Mining Countryside' both in the posthumous collection *Phoenix*. In the second volume (p. 106) of Nehls' composite biography is a report on Lawrence's own attitude to the novel. *A Casebook on 'Sons and Lovers'* (1969) edited by Gāmini Salgādo brings together a number of the essays mentioned above, together with some extracts from Lawrence's letters and some early critical comments.

Lawrence — commentaries

NUNTHORPE GRAMMAR SCHOOL LIBRARY, YORK